Now's the Time for Jesus!

Let's Go

Fishing

"He who wins

souls is wise."

Proverbs 11:30

Dedication
and Acknowledgments

This book is dedicated to God the Father and Jesus Christ my Savior, and the Holy Spirit.

This book is dedicated to all who read it and use it as a tool for Souls.

I dedicate this book to my loving husband Marty, who has been so faithful to encourage me and pray for me.

I acknowledge two wonderful and professional people, Pat McLaughlin and Pamela Thomas Mahaffey, who have worked countless hours preparing this book for the spreading of the Gospel of Jesus Christ....along with countless others (too many to list) who over the years have contributed towards this book through their ideas, prayers, financial support and encouragement.

Special thanks to Robin Art for many hours spent on the original painting which appears on the cover. Thanks also to Jim Art for his creative cover design.

Our heart's desire...

is that God will use all that **you** learn from reading this book to lead many to Jesus. God desires to use the anointing on you to reach the Lost!

We know that you have been praying for many friends, relatives, acquaintances, co-workers and neighbors, longing to see them know Jesus. Our prayer is that you will learn tools in this book that will help you reach these people and many others so they will have a personal relationship with Jesus.

Our heartfelt prayer is that you will continue to be a soul winner for the rest of your life. May joy fill your heart each day as you see souls coming to the Lord by your being a witness for Jesus Christ.

God bless you and remember Proverbs 11:30 – "He who wins souls is wise."

We love you,

Marty and Joan Pearce

Marty and Joan Pearce

TABLE OF CONTENTS

Introduction

Over twenty years ago God spoke to me about writing this book. At the time I could not read and could barely write. This book was and is a true miracle! God gets all the credit – to God be the Glory!

The Holy Spirit led me all along, having me scribble down notes and scripture references. Then I would sit with a close friend and dictate what I wrote. She organized what I did and helped get it set up for printing. Both *Let's Go Fishing* and *The Empty Spot* were written while I was illiterate.

As I was writing these books, God also told me to hold weekly home Bible studies. During the studies, He supernaturally taught me to read and led me into full-time ministry. I then went to Bible college and later received an honorary Doctor of Ministry degree from a Bible college.

From being obedient in small things, God increased the ministry to the point where I was sent to the nations – India, Mexico, the Philippines, Jamaica, and others, and to extensive work throughout America. The ministry teaches and trains in Bible colleges and minister's conferences.

My husband and I and our ministry teams also spearhead *God Is Taking A City* campaigns, a special kind of outreacch, described in Chapter 20 of this book. This is where churches come together to win their city for Jesus by doing a variety of outreaches.

We also do large and small revival meetings in tents and churches. We have seen countless notable miracles and have seen multitudes come to Jesus and be filled with the Holy Spirit.

Now God has also allowed us to be on television world-wide. Our ministry has an ongoing food and clothing programs which reach out to the poor and needy throughout the nations.

The vision of Channel of Love Ministries is to impact the whole world and fulfill the Great Commission.

The message of *Let's Go Fishing* is that "All are called" to preach the gospel. It answers the questions of why, when, where and how we are to evangelize. It teaches you how to evangelize Jesus' way. The Holy Spirit led me to hundreds of Scriptures as He oversaw the writing of this book.

He who wins souls is wise (Proverbs 11:30).
So... *Let's Go Fishing!*

May God bless you as you read *Let's Go Fishing!* and may you come to know your calling and fulfill it.

Evangelist Joan Pearce
President and Founder
Channel of Love Ministries International

Preface

At the beginning of each *Let's Go Fishing!* chapter you will notice a drawing of a fish. We've deliberately chosen all kinds of fish from many parts of the world. As you look at them, we want you to notice that though they are all called "fish", they clearly also have very different looks and characteristics.

We've put these fish in here to represent people – people all around the world, who have all kinds of looks and all kinds of customs. These are the people we have to go fishing for. The foreign fish mean we need to be doing missionary work for the Lord. Some of these fish represent people you work with. Others are people you come in contact with in your usual daily routines. This book will help you be an effective fisher of men.

Notice how soul winning has actual connections to when you go out fishing. When you go out to catch real fish, they usually don't want to bite the bait. And then, when that fish does bite the bait, it starts to fight to get loose. That's what makes fishing an exciting, interesting challenge, yet also fun.

Remember...

It takes patience to wait for that fish to give in and let you be able to pull it in.

A key to being a successful fisherman especially for family and loved ones, is that families will watch your life-style to see if they want to truly surrender to Jesus.

In fishing for all people: 1. Pray for them always. 2. Love will conquer everything. 3. Be a witness and use the tools in this book to share your faith.

God bless you, and **Let's Go Fishing!**

Chapter 1

Why Are We To Go Out Witnessing?

I. Jesus has called us to go.

Matthew 4:19-20 - Then He said to them, "Follow Me, and I will make you fishers of men." They immediately left their nets and followed Him.

Jesus wants us to go fishing for men so that they can come to know Jesus as their Lord and Savior.
> **1.** Fear stops us.
> **2.** Rejection from others or embarrassment hinders us.
> **3.** More love will cause us to reach out.

Matthew 9:35-38 - Then Jesus went about all the cities and villages, teaching in their synagogues, preaching the gospel of the kingdom, and healing every sickness and every disease among the people. But when He <u>saw</u> the multitudes He was <u>moved</u> with <u>compassion</u> for them, because they were weary and scattered, like sheep having no shepherd.
Then He said to His disciples, "The harvest truly is plentiful, but the laborers are few. Therefore <u>pray</u> the Lord of the harvest to send out laborers into His harvest."

We are to be like Jesus, who:
> **1.** <u>saw</u> - First, we must see the lost.
> **2.** <u>was moved</u> - We are to act upon what we see, by reaching and out and sharing Jesus.
> **3.** <u>had compassion</u> - We are to put love in action.

4. <u>prayed</u> - We are to pray that we will be soul-winners for Jesus and also that there will be more laborers.

Jesus told the disciples the world was lost and the people were like sheep without a shepherd. A sheep without a shepherd will wander away from the flock and get into trouble or wolves or other wild animals may kill it. Jesus gave many warnings about the dangers for those who are lost.

John 10:10 - "The thief does not come except to steal, and to kill, and to destroy. I have come that they may have life, and that they may have it more abundantly."

When the thief comes, he brings only trouble, making people feel:

1. Lost, forsaken, lonely
2. Sick
3. Depressed

II. Jesus sends people out.

A. Jesus sends forth all believers to preach the kingdom message.

Jesus recognized that He was sent out to preach the gospel. He said:

Luke 4:18 - "The Spirit of the Lord is upon Me, because He has anointed Me to preach the gospel to the poor; He has sent Me to heal the brokenhearted, to proclaim liberty to the captives and recovery of sight to the blind, to set at liberty those who are oppressed."

Jesus wants us to walk in the same authority.

John 14:12 - "Most assuredly, I say to you, he who believes in me, the works that I do he will do also; and greater works than these he will do, because I go to My Father."

When we are one with Jesus, in unity, we will see the miracles and see captives set free.

John 15:4-5 - "Abide in Me, and I in you. As the branch cannot bear fruit of itself, unless it abides in the vine, neither can you, unless you abide in Me. I am the vine, you are the branches. He who abides in Me, and I in him, bears much fruit; for without Me you can do nothing."

John 15:16 - "You did not choose Me, but I chose you and appointed you that you should go and bear fruit, and that your fruit should remain, that whatever you ask the Father in My name He may give you."

Mark 16:15-18 - "Go into the world and preach the gospel to every creature. He who believes and is baptized will be saved; but he who does not believe will be condemned. And these signs will follow those who believe: In My name they will cast out demons; they will speak with new tongues; they will take up serpents; and if they drink anything deadly it will by no means hurt them; they will lay hands on the sick and they will recover."

We must live in this world and be bold witnesses for Jesus. As He told His disciples, He also tells us today.

1. We are called to witness.

2. We are called into the ministry of reconciliation and are ambassadors for Christ.

2 Corinthians 5:20 - Now then, we are ambassadors for Christ, as though God were pleading through us; we implore you on Christ's behalf, be reconciled to God.

What are some of the things that ambassadors do?

1. They stand in place of (represent) another.

2. They speak for that person in his or her absence.

3. They have full authority (i.e. the power of attorney) for that person.

III. We are stewards of the Gospel.

We have been commanded to be good stewards of God's Word. Take time to read in the scriptures what Paul said about his stewardship of the Word.

Romans 1:16 - For I am not ashamed of the gospel of Christ, for it is the power of God to salvation for everyone who believes, for it is for the Jew first and also for the Greek.

This is our purpose for preaching: to bring people into the knowledge of what Jesus has done for them and to bring them into salvation.

Teach the Full Gospel

1. Salvation

John 3:16-17 - For God so loved the world that He gave His only begotten Son....

Romans 8:9-10 - If you confess with your mouth the Lord Jesus and believe in your heart that God has raised Him from the dead....

John 11:25 - "I am the resurrection and the life, He who believes in Me...."

Acts 2:21 - ...whoever calls on the name of the Lord shall be saved.

Philippians 2:10-11 - ...that at the name of Jesus every knee shall bow....

John 3:3 - Most assuredly, I say to you, unless one is born again, he cannot see the kingdom of God."

2. Healing

Matthew 10:7-8 - "And as you go, preach, saying: 'The kingdom of heaven is at hand.' "Heal the sick, cleanse

the lepers, raise the dead, cast out demons...."
Matthew 9:20-22 - "If only I may touch His garment, I shall be made well."
Mark 2:1-11 - "....I say to you, arise, take up your bed, and go your way to your house."
Matthew 8:1-3 - ....Then Jesus put out His hand and touched him, saying, "I am willing; be cleansed."

3. Deliverance
John 10:10 - "The thief does not come except to steal, and to kill, and to destroy. I have come that they may have life...."
Mark 1:2-6 - ....John came baptizing in the wilderness and preaching a baptism of repentance for remission of sins....
Mark 16:15-20 - "....And these signs will follow those who believe: In My name they shall cast out demons...."

4. Prosperity
Matthew 6:25 - "Therefore I say to you, do not worry about your life, what you will eat or about your body, what you will put on...."
Psalm 35:27 - ....and let them say continually, "Let the Lord be magnified, who has pleasure in the prosperity of His servant."
John 10:10 - "....I have come that they may have life, and that they may have it more abundantly."
3 John 2 - Beloved, I pray that you may prosper in all things and be in good health, just as your soul prospers.
Luke 12:32 - "Do not fear, little flock, for it is your Father's pleasure to give you the kingdom."

20

Chapter 2

Where Do We Start?

I. Sowing and Reaping - We Work Together.

When we go out witnessing to the world, we need to know with confidence that all we do and say is advancing the Kingdom of God.

> **John 4:34-38 -** Jesus said to them, "My food is to do the will of Him who sent Me, and to finish His work. Do you not say, 'There are still four months and then comes the harvest'? Behold I say to you, lift up your eyes and look at the fields, for they are already white for harvest! And he who reaps receives wages, and gathers fruit for eternal life, that both he who sows and he who reaps may rejoice together. For in this the saying is true: One sows and another reaps. I sent you to reap that for which you have not labored; others have labored, and you have entered into their labors."

Some Plant   **Some Water**

We are all working together!

1 Corinthians 3:4-9 - For when one says, "I am of Paul," and another, "I am of Apollos," are you not carnal? Who then is Paul, and who is Apollos, but ministers through whom you believed, as the Lord gave to each one? I planted, Apollos watered, but God gave the increase. So then neither he who plants is anything, nor he who waters, but God who gives the increase. Now he who plants and he who waters are one, and each one will receive his own reward according to his own labor. For we are God's fellow workers; you are God's field, you are God's building.

II. Are we all called?

Yes! We may all be at different levels of our spiritual growth, but God will use us right where we are, in the ministry of reconciliation, to bring people to a saving knowledge of Jesus.

We are **all** called, not just a few of us.

A. We all have talents and we must use them.
Matthew 25:14-15 - [Jesus said] "For the kingdom of heaven is like a man traveling to a far country, who called his own servants and delivered his goods to them. And to one he gave five talents, to another two, and to another one, to each according to his own ability; and immediately he went on a journey."

We have all received talents. We as children of God have talents. We are all at different levels of spiritual maturity, but God wants us to use the talents we have to minister to the world.

In Matthew 25, we see that the Lord departed for a journey, and he left his servants in charge to do something with the talents he gave them.

Jesus commissions us to take His Gospel to others, using the talents He has given to us!

We have been given talents, in order to bring in the harvest. Our talents include:

1. **Plowing** up the ground.
2. **Planting** the seed.
3. **Watering** the seed.
4. **Harvesting** the crop.
5. **Following through** with the crop.

Each talent we have been given is to be fully developed and used.

> **Matthew 25:16-18** - "Then he who had received the five talents went and traded with them, and made another five talents. And likewise he who had received two gained two more also. But he who had received one went and dug in the ground, and hid his lord's money."

Know Your Talents

What talents have you been given? List them below.

Talk relate Serve, food, work, Fellowship, Help people

Now that you have listed your talents, ask God how you can use each talent to evangelize.

Consider Your Testimony

Revelation 12:10-11 – "…Now salvation, and strength, and the kingdom of our God, and the power of His Christ have come, for the accuser of our brethren, who accused them before our God day and night, has been cast down. And they overcame him by the blood of the Lamb and by the word of their testimony…."

What is your testimony? Here are some things to help you prepare your personal testimony to be shared with others. Probably your testimony was serious and griev-ous before you accepted Jesus. Your new testimony should highlight your experience of what God did.

> **1. Give the credit to Jesus.** Share what Jesus did for you and give God praise and glory.
>
> **2. Use Scriptures.** Find ways to weave scriptures throughout what you share.
>
> **3. Include the Salvation message.** Seek to offer the person several ways and opportunities to come to Jesus, throughout the testimony you bring to them.

Now let's start to use our talents and testimony.

> **1.** We can all pass out tracts. Do you realize that 65% of all Christians come to the Lord as a result of reading a tract?
>
> **2.** We all have a testimony which we can share.

Remember: Use the talents God has given you. Start today. God will give you more talents in soul-winning as you go forth.

Do an Act of Love

Be a friend. Do yard work, clean a house, baby sit, take food to someone.

Sing out about Jesus at street concerts, nursing homes, and in parks.

Keep in contact. Write notes and emails to the lost, lonely and hurting. Send out tracts, books and other useful materials.

B. We will be rewarded according to what we do with the talents God has given to us.

Matthew 25:19-23 - "After a long time the lord of those servants came and settled accounts with them.

"So he who had received five talents came and brought five other talents, saying, 'Lord, you delivered to me five talents; look, I have gained five more talents besides them.' His lord said to him, 'Well done, good and faithful servant; you were faithful over a few things, I will make you ruler over many things. Enter into the joy of your lord.'

"He also who had received two talents came and said, 'Lord, you delivered to me two talents; look, I have gained two more talents besides them.' His lord said to him, 'Well done, good and faithful servant; you have been faithful over a few things, I will make you ruler over many things. Enter into the joy of your lord.'"

Consider what the lord said to the faithful servant. This is how it will be for those who are faithful to Jesus.

1. Jesus will say, "Well done, thou good and faithful servant."

2. Jesus will let you move into a bigger realm and use you more and more once you start out by faith.

3. Jesus will say, "Enter into the joy of your Lord."

The wicked servant did not use the talent his lord had given him.

Matthew 25:24-28 - "Then he who had received the one talent came and said, 'Lord, I knew you to be a hard man, reaping where you have not sown, and gathering where you have not scattered seed. And I was afraid, and went and hid your talent in the ground. Look, there what you have is yours.'

"But his lord answered and said to him, 'You wicked and lazy servant, you knew that I reap where I have not sown, and gather where I have not scattered seed, so you ought to have deposited my money with the bankers, and at my coming I would have received back my own with interest.

"Therefore take the talent from him, and give it to him who has ten talents."

<u>What is to be learned from the wicked servant?</u>
>**1.** Fear stopped him.
>**2.** He had no relationship with the lord. If he had, he would have known that the lord was good. Instead, the servant thought that the lord was a hard man.

From this story Jesus told, we need to learn that God loves us very much. He is looking for those with faithful and willing hearts. If we make mistakes when we are witnessing, or don't have all the know-how, God understands. He sees our faithfulness and the Holy Spirit will guide and teach us.

FEAR stopped the wicked servant from doing anything with his talent.

<u>Where does fear come from</u>? We can answer this by knowing where fear **does not come from.**

>**2 Timothy 1:6-8** – Therefore I remind you to stir up the gift of God which is in you through the laying on of my hands. For God hath not given us the spirit of fear, but of power, and of love, and of a sound mind. Therefore do not be ashamed of the testimony of our Lord, nor of me His prisoner, but share with me in the sufferings for the gospel according to the power of God.

Chapter 3

What Happens If We Don't Go Witnessing?

I. We have been called to become fishers of men.
   Let's talk about fishing.

I could have all the know-how available about fishing. I could have all the right fishing gear, including hooks, bait, weights and the best pole.

But if I put my pole in a bathtub filled with water, and fish all day, all week, and even all year, I'll never catch a fish.

   In order to catch a fish, we must go to where the fish are.

II. Where should we go fishing for souls?
   The lost are not usually found in churches. We must go out into the world to minister to the lost. Take time to read the following scriptures:

   Luke 19:2-10 - Jesus is a guest of Zacchaeus, a sinner.

   Luke 7:34 - Jesus is a friend of publicans and sinners.

   Matthew 9:10-13 - Jesus eats with publicans and sinners.

Fishing is "One on One!"

Luke 15:2-7 - Jesus receives sinners and eats with them.

And the Pharisees and scribes murmured, saying, "This man receives sinners and eats with them.

So He spoke this parable to them, saying: "What man of you, having a hundred sheep, if he loses one of them, does not leave the ninety-nine in the wilderness, and go after the one which is lost until he finds it?

"And when he has found it, he lays it on his shoulders, rejoicing. And when he comes home, he calls together his friends and neighbors, saying to them, 'Rejoice with me, for I have found my sheep which was lost!'

"I say to you that likewise there will be more joy in heaven over one sinner who repents than over ninety-nine just persons who need no repentance."

We must do as Jesus did. He went out to find the one that was lost.

Matthew 22:2-10 - "The kingdom of heaven is like a certain king who arranged a marriage for his son, and sent out his servants to call those who were invited to the wedding; and they were not willing to come.

"Again, he sent out other servants, saying, 'Tell those who are invited, "See, I have prepared my dinner; my oxen and fatted cattle are killed, and all things are ready. Come to the wedding."'

"But they made light of it and went their ways, one to his own farm, another to his business. And the rest seized his servants, treated them spitefully, and killed them.

"But when the king heard about it, he was furious. And he sent out his armies, destroyed those murders, and burned up their city.

"Then he said to his servants, 'The wedding is ready, but those who were invited were not worthy. **Therefore go into the highways**, and as many as you find, invite them to the wedding.'

"So those servants went out **into the highways** and gathered together all whom they found, both bad and good. And the wedding hall was filled with guests."

In this parable, the king sent his servants into the highways — where the people were. They were told to come, as many as the servants could find. He told them to **compel** the people to come in so that his house could be filled up.

We **must** do the same thing. Everywhere we go, on the streets, in restaurants, at the bowling alley, on the job and house-to-house, we must **compel** the people to come to Jesus.

Jesus Himself ministered in the street, on the hillsides, in the synagogues, and in the houses. He preached everywhere — to large groups as well as one-on-one.

In the Book of Acts, the apostles talked everywhere about Jesus. Paul ministered in jail, to the soldiers and to judges. He taught publicly and from house to house.

An evangelistic crusade is a great tool, which offers opportunity for many individuals to play a part. An evangelist

32

can come and do outreaches with the local church or churches and catch large numbers of converts — just like a fisherman catches many fish.

The early apostles saw large numbers come in at one time, as the church grew daily. Jesus talked to thousands at one time. In the Philippines, in India, as well as in the United States we at Channel of Love Ministries see large numbers come for salvation at one time.

Evangelistic Crusades need to be well organized. We must individually pray that God's Spirit will move mightily to bring souls to salvation. We can invite people to crusades, and offer to take them there. After they have committed their lives to Jesus, we must follow up, by teaching them the Word and getting them into a good church where they can grow in God.

Christian plays and concerts are also great ways to reach the lost.

Don't forget the children! Puppet shows, Christian movies, and sidewalk and summer Bible classes are all good ways to reach them.

Bible study outreaches are a wonderful way to reach your neighbors and friends. You can cover a large radius, going door to door to invite them to come. Be sure your studies are supervised by mature Christians, and that you ask your pastor about how to get the groups started.

Other outreach ideas include going to jails, nursing homes, senior citizen groups, hospitals, high schools, parks, bus and train stations, airline terminals, and anywhere else groups of people are gathered in one place. Use the internet, websites and email as evangelistic tools to get the gospel out.

Be sure to follow the example of the apostles, who earnestly prayed, individually and in groups, that doors would be opened for them to preach the gospel!

The world is out there, just waiting for us!

The Body of Christ **must** begin to move out for God and do as we have been commanded to do.

God's calling is clear!

III. What happens if we don't go fishing?

A. The hungry may feed on the wrong food. When a fish is hungry enough, it will bite at any hook or any bait. We must hold forth the right bait and hook to those who are spiritually hungry — the Words of Life.

B. The lost and lonely may follow the wrong leader. There's a lost world out there, with people who are oppressed and lonely. They don't know where to turn or who to turn to. They may follow anyone who shows them what seems to be love, attention and kindness.

C. Since the lost don't go where the truth is preached, they may never hear it. Since the lost don't come to church, if we don't go fishing they will never get to hear the Good News of the Gospel.

D. Others are recruiting the lost into cults. There are other fisherman out there in the world who are hooking people into various cults.

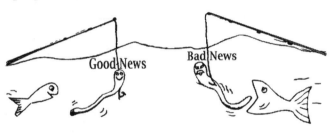

E. There are evil spirits and wrong doctrines in the world, which are drawing people away from truth.

We are in the last times. There are seducing spirits, doctrines of demons and humanistic doctrines and teachings which are running rampant in today's world. People are "having their consciences seared with a hot iron," and learning to care only about themselves.

> **2 Timothy 3:1-7** - But know this, that in the last days perilous times will come: For men will be lovers of themselves, lovers of money, boasters, proud, blasphemers, disobedient to parents, unthankful, unholy, unloving, unforgiving, slanderers, without self-control, brutal, despisers of good, traitors, headstrong, haughty, lovers of pleasure rather than lovers of God, having a form of godliness but denying its power. And from such people turn away! For of this sort are those who creep into households and make captives gullible women loaded down with sins, led away by various lusts, always learning and never able to come to the knowledge of the truth.

Today we see many people who are ever learning but never able to come to the knowledge of the truth. We need to be out where the sinners and the lost are. Because they are hurting they are reaching out and taking anything that comes their way!

2 Timothy 4:2-5 - Preach the word! Be ready in season and out of season. Convince, rebuke, exhort, with all longsuffering and teaching.

For a time will come when they will not endure sound doctrine, but according to their own desires, because they have itching ears, they will heap up for themselves teachers; and they will turn their ears away from the truth, and be turned aside to fables.

But you be watchful in all things, endure afflictions, do the work of an evangelist, fulfill your ministry.

Hebrews 13:9- Do not be carried about with various strange doctrines. For it is good that the heart be established by grace, not with foods which have not profited those who have been occupied with them.

Colossians 2:8 - Beware lest anyone cheat you through philosophy and empty deceit according to the tradition of men, according to the basic principles of the world, and not according to Christ.

Matthew 5:19 - Whoever therefore breaks one of the least of these commandments, and teaches men so, shall be called least in the kingdom of heaven; but whoever does and teaches them, he shall be called great in the kingdom of heaven.

Matthew 15:9 - "And in vain they worship Me, teaching as doctrines the commandments of men."

1 Timothy 1:4 - Nor give heed to fables and endless genealogies, which cause disputes rather than godly edification which is in faith.

1 Timothy 1:6-7 - From which some, having strayed, have turned aside to idle talk, desiring to be teachers of the law, understanding neither what they say nor the things which they affirm.

2 Peter 2:1-2 - But there were also false prophets among the people, even as there will be false teachers among you, who will secretly bring in destructive heresies, even denying the Lord who bought them, and bring on themselves swift destruction. And many will follow their destructive ways, because of whom the way of truth will be blasphemed.

Titus 1:11- Whose mouths must **be stopped**, who subvert whole households, teaching things which they ought not, for the sake of dishonest gain.

I marvel that you are turning away so soon from Him who called you in the grace of Christ, to a different gospel, which is not another; but there are some who trouble you and want to pervert the gospel of Christ.

Galatians 1:6-9

But even if we, or an angel from heaven, preach any other gospel to you than what we have preached to you, let him be accursed.

As we have said before, so now I say again, if anyone preaches any other gospel to you than what you have received, let him be accursed.

In Galatians, Paul has warned against receiving any other gospel except what he and the other apostles were teaching.

Ephesians 2:4-9- But God, who is rich in mercy, because of His great love with which He loved us, even when we were dead in trespasses, made us alive together with Christ (by grace you have been saved), and raised us up together, and made us sit together in heavenly places in Christ Jesus, that in the ages to come He might show the exceeding riches of His grace in His kindness toward us in Christ Jesus.

For by grace you have been saved through faith, and that not by yourselves; it is the gift of God, not of works, lest anyone should boast.

We are to take the message of the cross

What Jesus Did for Us ✝

to the world!

Galatians 1:10 - For do I now persuade men, or God? Or do I seek to please men? For if I still pleased men, I would not be a bondservant of Christ.

Like Paul, we are not to speak to please men, by telling them what they would like to hear. We must preach the truth.

Romans 1:16 - For I am not ashamed of the gospel of Christ, for it is the power of God to salvation for everyone who believes, for the Jew first and also for the Greek.

Chapter 4

Eight Steps on Moving in the Holy Spirit

1. The Holy Spirit is Power.

The Holy Spirit empowers us to be witnesses for Jesus.

Luke 24:49 - "Behold, I send the Promise of My Father upon you; but tarry in the city of Jerusalem until you are endued with power from on high."

Matthew 3:11 - "I indeed baptize you with water unto repentance, but He who is coming after me is mightier than I, whose sandals I am not worthy to carry. He will baptize you with the Holy Spirit and fire."

Acts 1:8 - "But you shall receive power when the Holy Spirit has come upon you; and you shall be witnesses to Me in Jerusalem, and in all Judea and Samaria, and to the end of the earth."

The church needed this infilling of the Holy Spirit so that they could be like Jesus and advance His kingdom.

Matthew 4:1 - Then Jesus was led up by the Spirit into the wilderness to be tempted by the devil.

Clearly, Jesus was led by the Holy Spirit.

Acts 10:38 - "...how God anointed Jesus of Nazareth with the Holy Spirit and with power, who went about doing good and healing all who were oppressed by the devil, for God was with Him."

We must also let the Holy Spirit flow through us, because we can do nothing without the power of the Holy Spirit.

Zechariah 4:6 - So he answered and said to me: "This is the word of the Lord to Zerubbabel: 'Not by might nor by power, but by My Spirit,' says the Lord of hosts."

II. The Holy Spirit makes us Bold.

Acts 2:1-4 - Now when the Day of Pentecost had fully come, they were all with one accord in one place. And suddenly there came a sound from heaven as of a rushing mighty wind, and it filled the whole house where they were sitting. Then there appeared to them divided tongues, as of fire, and one sat upon each of them. And they were all filled with the Holy Spirit and began to speak with other tongues, as the Spirit gave them utterance.

On the day that the early Church was born, the same apostles who had run and hidden when Jesus was crucified were filled with the power of the Holy Ghost. They went out and boldly proclaimed Jesus Christ.

Acts 2:14 - But Peter, standing up with the eleven, raised his voice and said to them, "Men of Judea and all who dwell in Jerusalem, let this be known to you, and heed my words."

Under the anointing of the Holy Spirit, Peter preached the great message from the prophet Joel, about the Spirit being poured out on all flesh. Notice how Peter's message cut into the hearts of his hearers.

Acts 2:36-38 - "Therefore let all the house of Israel know assuredly that God has made this Jesus, whom you crucified, both Lord and Christ." Now when they heard this, they were cut to the heart, and said to Peter and the rest of the apostles, "Men and brethren, what shall we do?" Then Peter said to them, "Repent, and let every one of you be baptized in the name of Jesus

Christ for the remission of sins; and you shall receive the gift of the Holy Spirit."

Because of the power and anointing of the Holy Spirit, three thousand were converted on that one day.

In Acts chapter 3, we see the great miracle of the man who was healed at the Beautiful Gate. That great miracle opened up opportunities for Peter to speak boldly to the multitudes, commanding them to repent and come to Jesus. Because of one miracle, five thousand souls were added to the Kingdom of God.

Next, we see the apostles arrested, and warned not to preach in the Name of Jesus.

Acts 4:19 - But Peter and John answered and said to them, "Whether it is right in the sight of God to listen to you more than to God, you judge."

Beloved, there is a day soon approaching when we will be in the same position as those in the early Church. When that time comes, we must continue to proclaim Jesus as they did.

And we should now also pray the same prayer those disciples prayed:

Acts 4:29-31 - "Now, Lord, look on their threats, and grant to Your servants that with all boldness they may speak Your word, by stretching out Your hand to heal, and that signs and wonders may be done through the name of Your holy Servant Jesus."

And when they had prayed, the place where they were assembled together was shaken; and they were all filled with the Holy Spirit, and they spoke the word of God with boldness.

The power of the Gospel is boldness with signs and wonders. We are to step out as believers and expect miracles.

> **Mark 16:15 -** And He said to them, "Go into all the world and preach the gospel to every creature."
>
> **1 Corinthians 12:7 -** But the manifestation of the Spirit is given to each one for the profit of all.

The manifestation of the Holy Spirit, through the gifts of the Spirit, is the tool for warfare in the advancement of the Kingdom of God. These gifts will operate as needed to reach the lost, sick and oppressed world.

When Jesus witnessed to the woman at the well in John Chapter 4, He operated in the Word of Knowledge and He discerned her past. Because of this gift operating through Jesus, the woman then became a believer. Through her testimony concerning her belief in Jesus, the entire town received Jesus as Lord.

The Gift of Healing is evidenced throughout the entire New Testament. The book of Acts is truly the account of signs and wonders through the operation of the Holy Spirit.

III. The Holy Spirit teaches us and helps us.

> **John 14:16 -** "And I will pray the Father, and He will give you another Helper, that He may abide with you forever...."
>
> **John 14:26 -** "But the Helper, the Holy Spirit, whom the Father will send in My name, He will teach you all things, and bring to your remembrance all things that I said to you.

When we are witnesses for Jesus, the Holy Spirit helps us by bringing to our remembrance the scriptures needed for each person. There are times when you're not sure what to say. Ask the Holy Spirit. He is our Helper. Talk to the Holy Spirit. He is always there to listen and to help us

> **Matthew 10:19-20 -** "But when they deliver you up, do not worry about how or what you should speak. For it

will be given to you in that hour what you should speak; for it is not you who speak, but the Spirit of your Father who speaks in you."

Let the Holy Spirit speak through us with an abundance of love for those to whom we witness, as a reflection of the Lord Jesus.

> **John 7:16 -** Jesus answered them and said, "My doctrine is not Mine but His who sent Me."
> **John 6:38 -** "For I have come down from heaven, not to do My own will, but the will of Him who sent Me." Let us yield ourselves to the Holy Spirit. Let His love work through us. We have the Word of Life so that others may receive Eternal Life.

IV. The Holy Spirit leads us.
Romans 8:14- For as many as are led by the Spirit of God, these are sons of God.

The Lord wants us to be led by the Holy Spirit. Pray and ask the Holy Spirit to lead you to lost and hurting people.

Acts 8:27 - So he [Philip] arose and went. And behold a man of Ethiopia, a eunuch of great authority under Candace the queen of the Ethiopians, who had charge of all her treasury, and had come to Jerusalem to worship, was returning.

Many times the Holy Spirit will lead you in stages, having you move out step by step. We see Philip in the desert, waiting for the Holy Spirit to direct his next step.

Acts 8:29-31 - Then the Spirit said to Philip, "Go near and overtake this chariot." So Philip ran to him, and heard him reading the prophet Isaiah, and said, "Do you understand what you are reading?" And he said, "How can I, unless someone guides me?" And

he asked Philip to come up and sit with him.
Then Philip shared Jesus with the man and he received
Jesus into his heart (vs. 35-39).

Another situation where the Holy Spirit led is in Acts
chapter 10. As Cornelius was in prayer, he was shown a
vision in which an angel told him to send for Peter. Mean-
while, in a city miles away, the Holy Spirit was speaking
to Peter through a vision.

> **Acts 10:19-20** - While Peter thought about the vision,
> the Spirit said to him, "Behold, three men are seeking
> you. Arise therefore, go down and go with them,
> doubting nothing; for I have sent them."

Peter listened, and obeyed the Holy Spirit. While he
was preaching at Cornelius' home, all those who were in
his household were saved and filled with the Holy Spirit.

In Acts chapter 16, we see that Paul is exhorted by the
Holy Spirit not to make a trip to Asia.

> **Acts 16:6** - Now when they had gone through Phrygia
> and the region of Galatia, they were forbidden by the
> Holy Spirit to preach the word in Asia.

Next we see the Holy Spirit again speaking, in a vision
given to Paul.

> **Acts 16:9-10** - And a vision appeared to Paul in the
> night. A man of Macedonia stood and pleaded with
> him, saying, "Come over to Macedonia and help us."
> Now after he had seen the vision, immediately
> we sought to go to Macedonia, concluding that the
> Lord had called us to preach the gospel to them

After following the Holy Spirit's leading to go
to Macedonia, Paul cast a demon spirit of divina-
tion out a servant girl. Then he and Silas were se-
verely punished and thrown in prison, where more
miracles happened. They were freed from their

chains and were able to convert their jailer and his whole household.

Take time to read Acts 16;10-34.

When we listen and obey the Holy Spirit and let the Spirit lead us, we always succeed. This is the way that we will see great signs and wonders.

V. The Holy Spirit convicts sinners and saints.

The lost need to hear the Good News that Jesus died for them. As we share God's anointed word, we have His promise about what the Word is and its power.

The Word of God

- will not return void, and will accomplish its purpose.

  Isaiah 55:11 - So shall My word be that goes forth from My mouth; it shall not return to Me void, but it shall accomplish what I please, and it shall prosper in the thing for which I sent it.

- is armor which helps us in warfare with the enemies of God.

  Ephesians 6:17 - And take the helmet of salvation and the sword of the Spirit, which is the word of God.

- is a powerful and cutting sword, which opens up deep things in those who hear it.

  Hebrews 4:12 - For the word of God is living and powerful, and sharper than any two-edged sword, piercing even to the division of soul and spirit, and of joint and marrow, and it is a discerner of the thoughts and intents of the heart.

We need to share the scriptures when we witness because the word of God is a sharp sword of His Spirit. It has power to pierce the heart of those with whom we are sharing the Gospel. We don't know the thoughts, hearts or desires of people, but God knows. God uses us as His voice for His purposes.

As you continue to go witnessing, the Spirit will teach you and show you which scriptures to share with each person. He knows each person's needs, and precisely which scriptures will draw them into hearing the Gospel message. When we speak under the anointing of the Holy Spirit mighty things will occur.

John 16:7-11 - [7] "Nevertheless I tell you the truth. It is to your advantage that I go away; for if I do not go away, the Helper will not come to you; but if I depart, I will send Him to you.

[8] And when He has come, He will convict the world of sin, and of righteousness, and of judgment: [9]of sin, because they do not believe me; [10]of righteousness, because I go to My Father and you see me no more; [11]of judgment, because the ruler of this world is judged."

It is the Holy Spirit, not you or me, Who convicts people:

Of Sin — Verse 9   **Of Righteousness** — Verse 10
Of Judgment — Verse 11

VI. The Holy Spirit helps us come to Christ.

A. <u>When the Spirit comes, He will convict the world of sin, and start working on the heart of the sinner.</u>

John 16:8 - "And when He has come, He will convict the world of sin, and of righteousness, and of judgment."

B. <u>To be "Born Again" we must confess Jesus as Lord.</u>

Romans 10:9-10 - "That if you confess with your mouth the Lord Jesus and believe in your heart that God has raised Him from the dead, you will be saved. For with the heart one believes unto righteousness, and with the mouth confession is made unto salvation."

C. No person can honestly say that Jesus is Lord except by the Holy Spirit.

1 Corinthians 12:3 - Therefore I make known to you that no one speaking by the Spirit of God calls Jesus accursed, and no one can say that Jesus is Lord except by the Holy Spirit

D. We are born again when we yield to the Spirit and receive Jesus as Lord over all areas of our lives.

John 3:5-8 - Jesus answered, "Most assuredly, I say to you, unless one is born of water and the Spirit he cannot enter the kingdom of God.

That which is born of the flesh is flesh, and that which is born of the Spirit is spirit.

Do you marvel that I said to you, 'You must be born again.'

The wind blows where it wishes, and you hear the sound of it, but cannot tell where it comes from and where it goes. So is everyone who is born of the Spirit."

E. The Spirit will witness with our spirit to the truth that we are the children of God.

Galatians 4:6 - And because you are sons, God has sent forth the Spirit of His Son into your hearts, crying out, "Abba, Father!"

Romans 8:14-17 - For as many as are led by the Spirit of God, these are sons of God.

For you did not receive the spirit of bondage again to fear, but you received the Spirit of adoption by which we cry out, "Abba, Father."

The Spirit Himself bears witness with our spirit that we are children of God, and if children, then heirs - heirs of God and joint heirs with Christ, if indeed we suffer with Him, that we may also be glorified together.

VII. The Holy Spirit is the assurance of our inheritance.

The Holy Spirit guarantees our inheritance in God.

Ephesians 1:13-14 - In Him you also trusted, after you heard the word of truth, the gospel of your salvation: in whom also, having believed, you were sealed with the Holy Spirit of promise, who is the guarantee of our inheritance until the redemption of the purchased possession, to the praise of His glory.

This guarantee is the inward and outward working of the Holy Spirit upon our lives, to draw us back on course in the event we start "drifting" from God.

1. When we grieve the Holy Spirit we must immediately repent and pray for restored fellowship with God.

1 Corinthians 3:16-17 - Do you not know that you are the temple of God and that the Spirit of God dwells in you? If anyone defiles the temple of God, God will destroy him. For the temple of God is holy, which you are.

2. We are to live a holy lifestyle before God, evidencing the fruit of the Spirit.

Galatians 5:22-25 - But the fruit of the Spirit is love, joy, peace, longsuffering, kindness, goodness, faithfulness, gentleness, self-control. Against such there is no law. And those who are Christ's have crucified the flesh with its passions and desires. If we live in the Spirit, let us also walk in the Spirit.

We are the temple of the Holy Spirit. Our bodies no longer belong to us. We are to live in love and obey God's Word. All the fruit of the Spirit should be apparent in our lives.

VIII. The Holy Spirit reveals.

   A. <u>The Spirit reveals deep things of God for us to share.</u>

     1 Corinthians 2:10-13 - But God has revealed them to us through His Spirit. For the Spirit searches all things, yes, the deep things of God.

     For what man knows the things of a man except the spirit of the man which is in him? Even so no one knows the things of God except the Spirit of God.

     These things we also speak, not in words which man's wisdom teaches, but which the Holy Spirit teaches, comparing spiritual things with spiritual.

   B. <u>The Spirit reveals mysteries of God's word to those who are born again.</u>

     Until we are born again, we can't understand the scriptures. "For the message of the cross is foolishness to those who are perishing, but to us who are being saved it is the power of God." (1 Corinthians 1:18). When we become born again through the blood of Jesus, we are brought into the kingdom of God. Then the Holy Spirit reveals the mysteries of God's Word.

     1 Corinthians 2:9 - But it is written: "Eye has not seen, nor ear heard, nor have entered into the heart of man the things which God has prepared for those who love Him." (See Isaiah 64:4 & 65:17)

     1 Corinthians 6:17 - But he who is joined to the Lord is one spirit with Him.

Because of our new birth, we must renew our mind, so that we are no longer conformed to the image of the world.

Romans 12:1-2 - I beseech you therefore, brethren, by the mercies of God, that you present your bodies a living sacrifice, holy, acceptable to God, which is your reasonable service.

And do not be conformed to this world, but be transformed by the renewing of your mind, that you may prove what is that good and acceptable and perfect will of God.

Chapter 5

How Do We Prepare Ourselves?

1. Soul winning will become easy as you get prepared.
    A. <u>Carefully study the lives of great soul-winners</u>.
Locate every book you can find on soul-winning and
evangelism. Read and meditate on them.

    B. <u>Learn the scriptures on soul-winning</u>. Mark these
scripture references in your Bible. Meditate on them
until they become part of you.
        2 Timothy 2:15 - "Be diligent (KJV - study) to present
yourself approved to God, a worker who does not
need to be ashamed, rightly dividing the word of
truth."

    **C. <u>Learn how to properly use the tools of witness-
ing, with love.</u>**
        2 Timothy 2:25-26 - ...in humility correcting those
who are in opposition, if God perhaps will grant
them repentance, so that they may know the truth,
and that they may come to their senses and escape
the snare of the devil, having been taken captive
by him to do his will.
    Don't argue. Just share the Word and the Word will
set them free.

11. We need to take the GOOD NEWS to the world.
    A. <u>Go forth in love.</u>
    **B. <u>Share about God's love for them, and what He
has done for them in Christ because of that love.</u>** It
is not necessary to tell them they are going to hell, but rather
tell them the GOOD NEWS, God's love for them.

52

C. <u>Share basic truths with them.</u> All have sinned and fallen short of the glory of God; the wages of sin is death, but the GIFT of God is eternal life through Jesus.

D. <u>Share how sin came into the world.</u> It came through Adam, who became separated from God through disobedience. Adam was not subject to sickness, poverty or death before the fall of man. What Adam lost was restored to us through the obedience of Jesus' dying on the cross and restoring mankind back to God.

E. <u>Share how Christ reconciled the world.</u> God was in Christ, reconciling the world to Himself, not counting men's sins against them, but canceling them.

F. <u>Share how we can be born again.</u> We can become new creations in Christ, children of God. We can obtain right standing with God.

III. We need to go out with the Wisdom of God.
1 Corinthians 1:30 - But of Him you are in Christ Jesus, who became for us wisdom from God—and righteousness and sanctification and redemption. When witnessing, pray that God's wisdom will flow through you.

Matthew 10:16 - "Behold, I send you out as sheep in the midst of wolves. Therefore be wise as serpents and harmless as doves."
A. Jesus related spiritual truths to the people using everyday language. With farmers he spoke of sowing and reaping; with fisherman he spoke of casting nets and catching fish.
We are to speak forth the words of life to the world using words people can understand. Our

53

words need to relate to the present time and to people's current situations.

B. Use familiar terminology, rather than church terminology. People who don't know Jesus don't understand your way of talking. Usually they can't relate to expressions such as: "Are you saved?" and "born again."

> **1 Corinthians 2:14** - For the natural man does not receive the things of the Spirit of God, for they are foolishness to him; nor can he know them, because they are spiritually discerned.

For example, many people think that because they've always gone to church, they're saved. They'll say: "I'm going to heaven. I never killed anyone, or stole anything. I'm a good person."

C. We need to be polite and tactful, yet firm.

> **1.** We need to be loving, yet certain we have something we need to share.
>
> > **Romans 5:5 -** ...because the love of God has been poured out in our hearts by the Holy Spirit who was given to us.

> **2.** We are to be lights in the world.
>
> > **Matthew 5:14-16 -** "You are the light of the world. A city that is set on a hill cannot be hidden.
> >
> > "Nor do they light a lamp and put it under a basket, but on a lampstand, and it gives light to all who are in the house.
> >
> > "Let your light so shine before men, that they may see your good works and glorify your Father in heaven."

3. We are to be salt in the earth.

> **Matthew 5:13 -** "You are the salt of the earth; but if the salt loses its flavor, how shall it be seasoned? It is then good for nothing but to be thrown out and trampled underfoot by men."

4. We need to use the Word of God. Remember, it is God's Word that will accomplish what He wants accomplished.

> **Isaiah 55:11 -** "So shall My word be that goes forth from My mouth; it shall not return to Me void, but it shall accomplish what I please, and it shall prosper in the thing for which I sent it."

IV. We need a prayerful and careful approach.

A. Be prayerful in your approach. You must be prayed up when you go out. Remain in an attitude of prayer, one of praying without ceasing.

1. Pray specifically that God will give you souls.

> **Colossians 4:3 -** ....meanwhile praying also for us that God would open for us a door for the word, to speak the mystery of Christ, for which I am also in chains.

2. Ask God to use you and give you a listener to witness to. The Lord will put people in your path.

3. Pray silently before you speak.

4. When working in teams, one person should pray and the other should share. Don't interrupt the flow of the Spirit by idle talk or unnecessary movements.

B. Be tactful in your approach.

1. Be friendly and polite.

2. Talk about things of interest to the person.

3. Let them express themselves. Don't do all the talking.

4. Watch your voice tone and body language.

5. Remember why you are approaching the person. Move on to the subject of salvation as soon as you can.

6. Be patient, but persistent. You are dealing with an eternal being, about a matter of life and death. We want them in the Kingdom of God.

7. Don't let them lead you off on tangents. Keep control of the conversation.

8. Don't debate with them. You are to present the Word to them and allow the Word to give them light.

C. Be aware of the importance of Timing.

1. It is ideal to approach people when they are alone, unrushed, and in a relaxed frame of mind. This can be done in such places as parks, airline terminals, and bus or train stations.

2. When going door to door, your approach must be quick and to the point. Introduce yourself, and then do something like the following:

Tell them, "We are in your neighborhood, seeking to find out how we can be of service in our community." Find out what their needs are and how you can help them. You can use the questionnaire in Appendix A.

There are many possible approaches. You may use different approaches at each house. Let the Lord guide you.

3. If you are witnessing in a park or restaurant etc., start your conversation by talking about something that is current in the news. Ask the Holy Spirit to help you bring your conversation to sharing eternal life. Ask the person these two most important questions:

> ▶ If you were to die tonight, do you know you would go to heaven?
> ▶ If you were standing before God and He asked you why He should let you into heaven, what would you say?

If the person's not sure, these questions will open them up. You'll know by their answers whether or not they have had a born again experience. If they haven't, ask them if you can share with them how they can have a personal relationship with Jesus. Then share the Gospel.

> ▶ If you are talking to people about Jesus, ask them if they have any prayer needs you can pray with them about.

After praying with them, ask them if they know for sure if they are going to heaven. Then share the Gospel, using the above approaches as a guide.

V. True love is the key to everything else.
Let's study what true love is.

The scripture tells us in 1 Corinthians 13:1-8,
Love is:
- ❤ longsuffering.
- ❤ kind.
- ❤ not puffed up.
- ❤ not provoked.

Love does not:
- ❤ envy.
- ❤ parade itself.
- ❤ behave rudely.
- ❤ seek its own.
- ❤ rejoice in iniquity, but rejoices in truth.

Love:
- ❤ thinks no evil.
- ❤ bears, believes, hopes, endures all things.

FROM 1 JOHN, CHAPTER 4

Beloved, let us love one another, for love is of God; and everyone who loves is born of God and knows God (V. 7).

Beloved, if God so loved us, we also ought to love one another (V. 11).

There is no fear in love; but perfect love casts out fear, because fear involves torment. But he who fears has not been made perfect in love (V. 18).

Prayer for Preparing
to Go Out Witnessing

Colossians 4:3-6 *³* ...meanwhile praying also for us, that God would open to us a door to the word, to speak the mystery of Christ, for which I am also in chains, *⁴*that I may make it manifest, as I ought to speak. *⁵*Walk in wisdom toward those who are outside, redeeming the time. *⁶*Let your speech always be with grace, seasoned with salt, that you may know how you ought to answer each one.

1. <u>Pray that God would open a door (v. 3)</u>. Pray that people will be open, with receptive hearts to hear what you have to say.

2. <u>Pray that you will speak the mysteries of Christ (v. 3)</u>. Pray that the Holy Spirit will lead your conversation.

3. <u>Pray that you will speak as you ought (v. 4)</u>. Pray that the Holy Spirit will put all the right words in your mouth and that the Holy Spirit will give you specific words. Ask for the gifts of the Holy Spirit needed for each individual, such as prophetic words of knowledge, etc.

4. <u>Pray that you will walk in wisdom (v. 5)</u>. Pray that you will walk in wisdom in small things and large things. This includes things such as your not being negative about anything, having the right tone of voice and body language, and being polite. It also involves being sensitive to those being witnessed to, including *their* moods, body language, situations and surroundings.

5. Pray that you will redeem the time (v. 5). *Be very aware when witnessing.* Satan will set up diversions to take up all your time so that you will miss talking to the right people, or coming to the important topics. Remember the mission is to talk about Jesus. Keep debates, idle conversations and distracting situations, no matter how important, to a minimum.

6. Pray that your speech will be seasoned with grace and salt (v. 6). Your speech is going to cover two subjects:**grace**-- God's unmerited favor, and **salt**-- which means preserving the simple purity of the word of God. Sensitivity to the Holy Spirit will show you how to mix the right combination of grace and salt in each conversation.

An Actual Example

I was witnessing to a couple. Everything was going great. It came to the point when it was time for them to make a decision to follow Christ. Then I asked them to ask Jesus to be their Lord and Savior. They paused and said they wanted to explain that they were living together and not married.

God's grace is that He wants <u>all</u> to be saved and it's not <u>by works</u>, but by faith in Jesus.

I stated that what they were doing in living together was against God's word. But God loved them and wanted them both saved. I stated that before they prayed to accept Jesus, they would have to make a decision based on the word of God to change their lifestyle and stop sinning. I did not condemn them. I just used the mixing of grace and salt together.

They both decided that they wanted to ask Jesus into their hearts. And then they prayed and received Jesus into their heart, and asked God to forgive their sin. Then they made arrangements so one would sleep on the sofa and the other in the bedroom.

Within a week the couple were married and they are serving God as a powerful team. It was love the sinner, but hate the sin.

7. <u>Pray you will know how to answer each one (v. 6)</u>. By spending quality time in prayer you will become sensitive to the Holy Spiri, and the Holy Spirit will speak through you.

Remember 2 Timothy 2:15
Be diligent to present yourselves
approved to God,
a worker who does not need to be ashamed,
rightly dividing the word of truth.

Notes and Reflections

Chapter 6

Love In Action

We are the most fortunate generation to live on this great planet earth.

We are the Ones!
The End Time Harvesters!

We must do what God has commanded us, and what Jesus told us to do.

Love your neighbor as yourself!

I. Love.

[Jesus said,] "This is My commandment, that you love one another as I have loved you." (John 15:12)

We are to love:

1. The sinner.
2. The drug addict.
3. The prostitute.
4. The person we can't stand to be with.
5. The person who hurts us.
6. The unlovely.
7. The one who is our enemy. (Pray for your enemies and get them saved.)

God's love in your heart will compel you to share with all people. Love them ALL. As you share, God's heart cry will come from deep inside of you.

II. Pray.

Ask God to put people in your path to witness to each day.
Pray Each Day:

1. "God, give me your heart for the lost."

2. "God, let me be a vessel of your love."

3. "God, give me compassion for others."

Remember: Be aware of the world around you! Talk to people: in stores, in restaurants, at bus stops, in parks, at the post office, on the streets, everywhere you go.

Plant seeds of Jesus' love.

Prayer is so crucial to being an effective soul winner. Everyone who comes into the kingdom of God is a result of someone's intercession. ***PRAY!***

III. Follow Through.

1. Take time to follow up on everyone you are responsible for leading to the Lord.

2. Pray that Christ be formed in them.

3. Take time to teach them, in a small Bible study.

4. Take them to church.

5. Visit them or give them a phone call.

6. Keep in touch with them often, so that the seeds planted can take root.

Never Get Discouraged!

When you're soul-winning don't ever get discouraged. Some souls will take months or even years of being witnessed to, before they make a commitment.

▸ God won't give up on them, so neither should we.

▸ Love will keep you going back, time after time.

▸ Remember that you are dealing with an eternal life.

Don't Be Moved by What you See!

Often outward actions and appearances are a person's way to cover up what's really happening in their heart. People have many ways of covering up what's deep inside them.

Remember the woman who washed Jesus' feet? She was a hard-looking person, but Jesus looked INSIDE her heart! We must never be moved by outward appearances.

<u>Know this for certain</u>: God is working on the heart!

Keep on planting seed!
Sooner or later
they will come to Jesus!
♥ Remember to Love - Love - Love! ♥

We want all to come to make a commitment to Jesus.

Romans 10:9-10 tells how one may receive Christ, and thus become a child of God:

"...if you confess with your mouth the Lord Jesus Christ and believe in your heart that God has raised Him from the dead, you will be saved.

"For with the heart one believes unto righteousness, and with the mouth confession is made unto salvation."

66

Salvation is a heart affair. A person believes in their heart and confesses with their mouth. When they do this, God gives them Eternal Life. The Word of God that they have acted upon is their evidence of salvation.

Joy may come as a result of being saved, but **the real evidence of salvation is the Word of God** which says, "if you confess with your mouth" and "believe in your heart" you are saved!

Notes and Reflections

The Church on the Move!

The boat steering wheel shows the church in motion. The Holy Spirit will birth ministry in the local church to do various outreaches and discipleship endeavors. This will result in church growth.

Chapter 7

Outreaches

Evangelistic Outreach is the Church in motion, reaching out to the lost and hurting so that they will come to Jesus. There are almost limitless possibilities for outreaches. Some are included on our wheel. Here are a few others, with space for you to list even more!

Sports Events   Plays/Skits
Dinners   Healing Rooms
Puppets   Clothing/Food Ministry
TV/Radio   Counseling Services
Concerts   Missions
Teen Clubs   Prison Ministry
Intercessory Prayer Music Ministry
Hospitals   Nursing Homes

_____ _____
_____ _____
_____ _____

I. EVANGELISM

1. The church should have printed forms available for use in evangelism outreach. Members can use these to refer the names of friends and relatives for follow up by someone on the evangelism team. Trained team members should be available, on request, to go out and share the good news of the Gospel.

2. Door-to-door evangelism is very valuable. There can be regularly scheduled meetings, once or twice a month, of churches doing the Adopt-a-Block program (see chapter 14). Or those going into the surrounding areas can get together on a regular basis.

<u>Below is a suggested format for group evangelism outreaches.</u>
   a. Prayer.
   b. A 15-20 minute teaching on evangelism, so that the believers can be rooted and grounded on the basics of witnessings.
   c. Participants go out witnessings in teams, returning to church for prayer and closing.

The converts brought in through this outreach should be informed about available Bible studies and invited to attend a good Word church. Most importantly someone should be delegated to be responsible for follow up visits with each convert, so that they will all be encouraged in their faith.

3. Other forms of evangelism are telephone calling and mailing out tracts. Believers who aren't in a position to be able to go out witnessing, for example mothers with small children, can do these kinds of things. Using names and addresses from the phone book, send out notes in which you include questions 5 and 6 from the questionnaire in Appendix A. Tell them someone from the church will call them within a few days. Have people also assigned to do the contacts, and share the love of Jesus with them. This is a way to work for the Lord out of one's home.

4. Believers can also be assigned to minister in jails, prisons and juvenile homes on a one-to-one basis. These people can also organize Bible studies in the prisons and homes. Believers would be commited to this ministry by keeping in touch and spiritually guiding the people as long as possible. Once they leave the prison or jail, it's important to keep them in our prayers. An effort should also be made to get them into a good follow-up program.

II. PRAYER GROUPS

Prayer groups are the most important part of the ministry. All other groups need to keep this group informed about the dates and times of their outreaches. That way there will be intercessory prayer going on during the time of each ministry activity.

The names and needs of new converts should be given to the prayer warriors. Prayers such as those found in Ephesians 1:17-20 and Matthew 6:19 can be prayed for the new believers.

> **Ephesians 1:17-20 -** That the God of our Lord Jesus Christ, the Father of glory, may give to you the spirit of wisdom and revelation in the knowledge of Him, the eyes of your understanding being enlightened; that you may know what is the hope of your calling, what are the riches of the glory of His inheritance in the saints, and what is the exceeding greatness of His power toward us who believe, according to the working of His power which He worked in Christ when He raised Him from the dead and seated Him at His right hand in the heavenly places.
>
> **Matthew 16:19 -** "And I will give you the keys of the kingdom of heaven, and whatever you bind on earth will be bound in heaven, and whatever you loose on earth will be loosed in heaven."
>
> **Colossians 4:12 -** Epaphras, who is one of you, a bondservant of Christ, greets you, always laboring fervently for you in prayers, that you may stand perfect and complete in all the will of God.

III. HOSPITALS

Members can refer sick friends and relatives to the church. A ministry group will be available to send pairs of people to hospitals to pray for the sick, lead them to the Lord and faithfully go and read the Word to them. This group can also reach out to shut-ins, the elderly and others who can't easily leave their homes to come to services.

The church should develop and keep an updated list of those needing home visitation.

Take some of these people on occasional outings. Most importantly, lead them to Jesus and read the Word to them on a regular basis.

IV. NURSING HOMES

Teams can be sent with musical instruments and singers. Have a time of praise and worship songs, followed by prayer, and a special message of the Gospel. The ministry leader should plan a scheduled time for these visits. In addition there can be one-on-one ministry, so that each person can know that they are truly loved and Jesus cares for them.

V. SOME OTHER MINISTRIES

The chart at the beginning of this chapter lists many kinds of evangelistic ministries. These ministries need to be connected together, as spokes are connected to a wheel. The goal is to have something that is moving and active. The church needs to move out to everyone who is unsaved. In order for this ministry wheel to travel throughout the world, there must be prayerfully organized and structured outreaches, as the Spirit of God moves upon the hearts of the leaders. The purpose of the outreach is to enable every church member who truly wants to step out in faith and evangelize to do so.

Believers have a variety of giftings and talents. Some people are creative and artistic and can make gifts for the sick and those in nursing homes. Others are active and out-going. They may want to contact new converts and give them rides to church services and activities. As the ministry grows, there may even be a need for a bus ministry to transport new converts.

As people are faithful about doing small things, God will see their faithfulness and use them more and more. We are all part of God's Army, and God wants all believers to enlist and to have all saved.

1 Timothy 2:3-4 - For this is good and acceptable and good in the sight of God our Savior, who desires all men to be saved and come to the knowledge of the truth.

Jesus is coming soon. His great commision is to reach the lost everywhere. Let us be doers of the Word and not hearers only.

James 1:22 - But be doers of the word, and not hearers only, deceiving yourselves.

Now is the time to possess the land for Jesus.

Having a food ministry is an excellent accompaniment to witnessing ministry. If a need comes up we can feed the poor as Jesus asked us to do. We can also take food baskets to the needy and be a blessing to them throughout the year as well as at holiday times.

Assign someone from the church to be responsible for and in charge of a clothing ministry. This ministry could be done at the church or from someone's home. Some guidelines are on the form in this chapter.

When needs come up, we will be able to bless the poor and those who are struggling with the things they need.

Matthew 25:35-40 - "For I was hungry and you gave Me food; I was thirsty and you gave Me drink; I was a stranger and you took Me in;

I was naked and you clothed Me; I was sick and you visited Me; I was in prison and you came to Me.

"Then the righteous will answer Him, saying, 'Lord, when did we see You hungry and feed You, or thirsty and give You drink?

'When did we see You a stranger and take You in, or naked and clothe You?

'Or when did we see You sick, or in prison, and come to You?'

"And the King will answer and say to them, 'Assuredly, I say to you, inasmuch as you did it to one of the least of these My brethren, you did it to Me.'"

The following are some tried and practical guidelines for doing a food and clothing ministry. These forms can be duplicated and used for handouts.

Notes and Reflections

FOOD MINISTRY

Fellowship name:_____

Bring food to:_____

Dates/Times:_____

Some Suggestions and Guidelines

1. If possible, choose cans, boxes and plastic containers (rather than glass jars)

2. Watch for store sales and coupon specials. Choose things you like to eat.

3. DO NOT BRING: dented cans, opened packages, perishable foods, highly sugared foods or juice drinks, soda, or junk foods.

4. Extra bags, boxes and large food storage bags are needed for delivery.

Below is a list of some suggested foods. Many other choices are possible, within these general areas.

MILK Canned condensed and evaporated milk, infant formula.

PROTEIN Canned meatballs, ham, chicken, turkey, beef stew, corned beef, tuna, salmon, hash, sardines, nuts.

VEGETABLES Cans of string beans, peas, spinach, collard greens, corn, beets, kidney beans, carrots, tomatoes, spaghetti sauce, sauerkraut, canned potatotes, yams.

STARCHES Canned pork & beans and corn, rice, spaghetti, macaroni, egg noodles, dry beans or peas, macaroni and cheese dinners.

JUICES Quarts of orange, grapefruit, cranberry, grape, tomato or apple juice (or individual packets of same). NO glass bottles or sugary juice drinks please!

LUNCH FOODS Peanut butter, jelly, canned soups, packaged soups, crackers, canned ravioli, spaghetti, macaroni and cheese.

CEREALS Packaged oatmeal, cream of wheat, farina, dry low-sugar cereals.

FRUITS Canned fruits (prefer light syrup); dried and unsweetened fruits such as raisins and prunes.

STAPLES Flour, sugar, salt, pepper, salt substitute. Basic spices such as: cinnamon, onion flakes, garlic powder, etc. Vanilla. Mayonnaise, mustard, ketchup, cooking oil.

NON-FOOD ITEMS *The following are not covered by food stamps*: Soap, toilet paper, toothpaste, laundry detergent, shampoo, paper towels, paper napkins, paper cups, feminine products, **disposable diapers**, facial tissues.

REMINDER: All kinds of non-perishable items and canned goods are good to keep on hand.

CLOTHING MINISTRY

We want to bless people with good quality new and used clothing.

To help us do this in the best way, we ask you to follow the guidelines and suggestions given here.

1. Clothing should be appropriate to the season. We do not have room to store out of season items. Please put out of season items aside for us.

2. Clothing MUST be clean, pressed, mended and ready to wear.

3. If it's out of style and/or you hate it — don't bring it! Avoid any clothing with inappropriate decals or designs.

4. Bring clothing on hangers (as appropriate), or neatly folded and sorted as to size.

5. NEW CLOTHING is especially welcome. Look for sales, end of season specials, close-outs, etc. Stop at garage sales. Buy an occasional gift for a needy person as you would for a member of your family. They are family too.

6. Especially needed are: shoes (particularly for children); baby and children's clothing; children's underwear and socks; men's clothing; larger size clothing for men, women and children.

7. Other needs are: sweaters, robes, and comfortable loose-fitting clothes for shut-ins and those in nursing homes and care centers.

8. We can also use winter clothes, coats, sweaters, blankets, hats, gloves, and sleeping bags for the homeless.

Bring Clothing to:_____

Days / Times to Bring Clothing:_____

Chapter 8

Saturday Soul-Winning Day

A Saturday soul-winning day is an excellent way to do soul-winning with members of a church or group of churches. People meet at the church or an arranged place for prayer and a brief study time. Then they go out street witnessing, usually in pairs.

Evangelists and intercessors are a key part of this effort. One of their primary roles is to see to it that the experience stays focused and well organized. Several things are necessary to keep this kind of ongoing activity effective and successful.

1. <u>Meet at the church</u> or other pre-arranged place.

2. Open with a time of <u>prayer</u>.

3. Have a 20 to 30 minute <u>study time</u> on soul-winning.
    a. Present scriptures on ways of witnessing.

    b. Do <u>role-playing</u>. Give out handouts with soul-winning situations. Have one person play the part of the one needing salvation and another the one witnessing to them.

    c. It's good to <u>practice using experienced leaders</u>, so that real kinds of situations can be shared and discussed.

4. <u>Pair up partners</u> to go out.
    a. The best combination is a man and a woman. This avoids situations such as having two men

knock on a door where a woman is home alone and might feel uncomfortable or even threatened.

b. Husband and wife teams are great.

c. Whenever possible, pair up experienced soul-winners with those who are inexperienced, or appear to be timid about going out.

5. Have everyone gather in teams for prayer. Allow time for each team to pray together.

6. Pray about where to go. Have a map of the city on the wall, with a sign over it saying, "Possess the land." Color in each area where you have sent teams. Place a red pin on the areas each time there is a salvation. Place a yellow pin where there is a baptism with the Holy Spirit. Place a green pin where a home Bible study is set up. This is a great visual aid, plus a wonderful way to encourage other church members to join the soul-winning team.

A Format for Going Out Witnessing

1. <u>Dress appropriately</u>. You want to be comfortably dressed for the weather, for walking and for the situation you'll be in, such as going to a park or visiting door to door. If you're going to a park, the women could wear nice pant outfits, and the men could wear slacks and a nice shirt. Be neat. Remember you represent Christ.

2. <u>If going door to door</u>, step back a step or two after knocking, so the occupant can open the door. Introduce yourself and the person with you. Though you may feel nervous, it is important the one opening the door see a big smile on your face. Speak with enthusiasm.

3. <u>Invite yourself in.</u> Ask if you could come in for just a few minutes, because you have something wonderful to share with them.

a. You might bring a short questionnaire. (See Appendix A). Say, "We have a short questionnaire that will help us learn how we can reach out to you and others in your neighborhood. Could we come in? This will only take a few minutes."

b. Most people will let you in. If they are in a hurry or not interested, briefly explain why you are out. Give them a tract to read, and let them know God loves them. Ask if they'd be willing to have you come back at a more convenient time. Make a note of that time and go back to them.

c. If they ask you in, be aware of the time. Remember you said you'd only take a few minutes. You will know by the Spirit if you are to stay longer.

4. <u>Once inside the home</u>, don't just go sit down. Wait for them to invite you to sit. If their suggested seating arrangement seems awkward, ask if you can sit closer to them. You want to be near enough so they can follow along as you read scriptures to them. Also you may want to have them read certain scriptures aloud.

5. <u>Have one person do the talking, while the other team member prays silently</u>. Pray quietly and seek to buffet all distractions while the witnessing is going on. For instance you might hold a crying baby, or head off a toddler seeking their parent's attention.

6. <u>If the TV or stereo is too loud</u>, politely ask if it could be lowered for a few minutes.

7. <u>Have a preset time when all the witnessing teams return to their gathering place</u>. Allow time for sharing experiences, highlighting what they learned and a time of prayer for all those who were ministered to during the outreach.

8. <u>Before people leave, have them fill out a follow-up card.</u> See a sample referral card in Appendix B. Make copies of the card for the worker, the intercessory prayer leader, and the church office.

The church should keep these records on file, in case a worker misplaces someone's name or phone number. Keeping good follow-up records emphasizes that everyone in the church understands that people's souls are involved in this work.

9. <u>Mail a personal note.</u> Have a supply of small blank greeting cards. Before they leave, have each team write short personal notes to those they visited. The notes should thank people for their time and let them know they will be prayed for. Be led by the Spirit to include scriptures and any specific comments. These notes are a way of blessing them. See Chapter 13, The 48 Hour Principle.

10. <u>The church response.</u> Have the church invite them to services. The note should also thank them for letting church members come and talk with them.

11. <u>Phone call follow up.</u> It is wonderful if someone from the church contacts those visited to see how they are. Encourage them to visit the church and offer a ride if needed. The idea is to reach out in kindness and love.

Notes and Reflections

Chapter 9

Taking People Through
The Scriptures

There are many different ways to share scriptures, as the Lord leads. This is the method I most commonly use.

1. Right from the start I tell them <u>we are not promoting a church or a program</u>.

2. We are <u>sharing Jesus and a relationship with Him</u>.

3. I say: "I would like to share what Jesus Himself said we must do to go to heaven."

John 3:1-8 - There was a man of the Pharisees named Nicodemus, a ruler of the Jews. This man came to Jesus by night and said to Him, "Rabbi, we know that You are a teacher come from God; for no one can do these signs that You do unless God is with him."

Jesus answered and said to him, "Most assuredly, I say to you, unless one is born again, he cannot see the kingdom of God."

Nicodemus said to Him, "How can a man be born when he is old? Can he enter a second time into his mother's womb and be born?"

Jesus answered, "Most assuredly, I say to you, unless one is born of water and the Spirit, he cannot enter the kingdom of God.

"That which is born of the flesh is flesh, and that which is born of the Spirit is spirit.

"Do not marvel that I said to you, 'You must be born again.'

"The wind blows where it wishes, and you hear the sound of it, but cannot tell where it comes from and where it goes. So it is with everyone who is born of the Spirit."

4. I say, "Nicodemus asked, 'What must I do to inherit the kingdom of God?'" Then I ask the person what they think the kingdom of God is, and where it's located. They usually tell me it's in heaven, but if they don't, I say, "Heaven."

5. I tell them what being born again means.
"You were born into this world through your mother's womb, through water." That is your natural birth.
I explain, "Man is spirit, soul and body; and this body will die and be buried. But the spirit part of a person goes on. It goes to either heaven or hell, according to the decision made here on earth. So Jesus is talking about a spiritual birth."

6. Then I go to scripture:
John 3:16 - "For God so loved the world that He gave His only begotten Son, that whoever believes in Him should not perish but have everlasting life."
I tell them, "God loved the world so much that He sent His only begotten Son, Jesus, to come and save us. That was so WHOEVER believes on Him should be saved."
I ask them what they think "whoever" means. Then I emphasize it means whatever they look like, "rich, poor, young, old - everyone. It means you and me."
I tell them that Jesus didn't come to condemn the world, but to save it. Then I read:
John 3:17 - "For God did not send His Son into the world to condemn the world, but that the world through Him might be saved."
I give an example to explain the meaning of the word "saved". "Suppose a little boy was standing on a road and a truck was about to run over him. If I run out and grab the

child off the highway, I have saved him from being run over. Or suppose someone pulls a toddler away from a hot, flaming fireplace. They've saved the child from being burned."

I tell them that Jesus is saving us from eternal punishment, or hell. When we confess Jesus as Lord and follow Him, we become children of God and have eternal life with Him.

I explain that we have no right to judge one another, because Romans 3:23 states that all have sinned. I tell them, "I have sinned, but Jesus washes me clean."

> **Romans 3:23** - For all have sinned and fall short of the glory of God.

When sharing with people, tell them that we all have sinned, except Jesus, and they nailed Him to the cross.

7. Then I read Romans 6:23:

> **Romans 6:23** - For the wages of sin is death, but the gift of God is eternal life in Christ Jesus our Lord.

Tell them that the wages of sin is death; but the gift of God is eternal life which comes through Jesus.

Then I use an example to explain what a gift is. "If I gave you a nicely wrapped package and then asked you to give me twenty dollars for it, would that be a gift? Or if I offered you the package and said you could keep it, but only if you came and mowed my lawn or cleaned my house, would that be a gift?"

I explain that a gift is free. When you get a gift you just receive it and say, "Thank You." That's how easy it is to receive Jesus.

Next, I take them to Ephesians 2:8-9:

> **Ephesians 2:8-9** - For by grace you have been saved through faith, and that not of yourselves, it is the gift of God, not of works, lest anyone should boast.

I tell them that salvation can't be earned! "We can't buy it! It is a free gift. You just receive it by faith!"

8. Then I turn to Romans 10:9-10:

> **Romans 10:9-10 -** ...that if you confess with your mouth the Lord Jesus and believe in your heart that God has raised Him from the dead, you will be saved. For with the heart one believes unto righteousness, and with the mouth confession is made unto salvation.

Note: I bring a Bible with me, in which I have highlighted scriptures related to salvation and the baptism with the Holy Spirit. Salvation scriptures are highlighted in red, and Holy Spirit scriptures in yellow. Then it's easy for me to find the highlighted sections.

9. Sometimes I define the word *Lord*. A lord is someone to whom we submit ourselves. We are to surrender our lives to Jesus as our Lord and Savior.

10. <u>The prayer to receive Jesus</u>.

When it's time for the closing prayer, I say to the person, "Let me see your hands." Then I take their hands in mine. After speaking with them quietly and giving them a few moments to relax, I tell them, "I am going to pray with you."

Note: Most people are nervous at this time. They may never have prayed before or be unsure about how to pray.

I say, "Don't be nervous. When I prayed this prayer, I didn't know what to say. I will pray, and you just repeat what I say."

Before starting the prayer, I tell them, "God is a spirit and He is here with us now, listening to our prayers."

Then I have everyone close their eyes.

Note: I keep my eyes open, and watch the person who is praying. If they are not repeating the prayer after me, I stop and start over, saying, "Come on; repeat after me."

I ask the team member with me to join in repeating the prayer with the new convert.

11. __The following points should be included in the Prayer:__

a. I am sorry for my sins (see Chapter 11, Godly Repentance).
b. I believe Jesus died for me and rose again from the dead.

c. Jesus, come into my life. I will make you ruler of my life from this day forward, and I will follow you.

d. If you know the person has been involved with the occult, witchcraft or drugs, have them renounce these things.

e. Have them say, "I am saved. Thank you, Jesus, for dying for me and saving me."

12. After praying with them, I read to them:
2 Corinthians 5:17 - Therefore, if anyone is in Christ, he is a new creation; old things have passed away; behold all things have become new.
2 Corinthians 5:21 - For He made Him who knew no sin to be sin for us, that we might become the righteousness of God in Him.

13. I ask them to get their Bible, if they have one. Inside the front cover I have them write, "I [their name] received Jesus as my Lord and Savior, to follow and obey from this day forward, on [date]." I explain that this is their birth certificate. If they don't have a Bible, we want to bring them one at another time, so we can start discipling them.

Then I discuss their status as a newborn baby in God's family. "If you had a new baby son and didn't give him milk to drink, what would happen to him?" They answer, "He would die."

Then I say, "Suppose you planted some flower seeds, and never watered them. What would happen?" Again they answer, "They would die."

Then I explain that a seed was just planted in them. Now, just as a new baby needs milk or a flower seed needs water, in order to live, they, the newborn Christian need certain things in order to survive and grow up in their spiritual life. The Bible, the book they have just written in, is the Word of God. It is their roadmap to success as a Christian.

14. Other things to do with the new convert before leaving them.

1. Tell them you would like to be their friend and help them learn the Bible.

2. Find out what day and time is most convenient and least hectic for them, and make an appointment to come and show them how to study the Word of God. Plan for weekly Bible Studies, lasting 30 to 40 minutes.

3. Write down the meeting date in your appointment book.

4. Make careful note of their name, address, phone number and any other important information.

5. Give them a small book as a gift, to encourage them. I usually give them a copy of my booklet "The Empty Spot," which explains the new birth. Inside the cover I write my name and number, my team member's name and number, and the date and time of our Bible Study.

6. The team member and I both welcome the person into the family of God.

7. We let them know they can call us for help of any kind. This includes things like needing a ride, or clothing or food. We will find a way to help them.

8. We share with them the importance of finding a good church and ask them to come to church with us. Some new converts are excited about going to church and will start going right away. However many people are timid after their conversion, and take their time about wanting to attend church. It is so important to do follow up and to disciple new converts.

Immediately set up a Bible Study, using a week-to-week plan. Channel of Love Ministries materials are very effective and have been used for years.

Now's The Time Bible Studies presents 12 lessons covering the basics of the Christian Faith. See Chapter 15 and the order/information form in the back of this book for details. Start teaching them in a weekly Bible Study.

Chapter 10

Key Soul-Winning Topics

I. Soul-Winning.
Questions to Ask.
1. If you were to die right now, do you know for sure that you would go to heaven?

2. Suppose you died and were standing before God. If He asked you why He should let you into Heaven, what would you say?

3. Could I take a moment to share with you, so that you can be sure what would happen if you were to die?

II. Salvation.
1. Every person must be born again to know God and have everlasting life (John 3:3; John 3:16).

2. The reason why we must be born again is found in Romans 3:23 (all have sinned).

3. Romans 6:23 - For the wages of sin is death, but the gift of God is eternal life in Christ Jesus our Lord.

4. Being saved or born again is receiving Jesus as your Lord (Master) and committing yourself to follow His Word (Romans 10:9-10).

5. Ask person if they believe that Jesus died for them and that God raised Jesus from the dead. If they believe these two things they can be saved.

6. Ask to take person's hand. Bow your head in prayer. YOU pray. Ask them to pray with you. (They repeat a phrase-by-phrase prayer after you.)

7. Pray this prayer with them:
> Jesus, I ask You to come into my life. I confess with my mouth that Jesus is my Lord. I believe in my heart that God has raised Jesus from the

dead. I turn my back on sin. I repent of all my sins. I am now a child of God. Thank you Jesus for saving me.

8. <u>Tell them to tell someone else about their salvation experience</u>. "Now tell someone today that you received Jesus as your Savior."

III. Sinners in Need of a Savior.
1. John 10:10 - <u>"The thief does not come except to steal, and to kill, and to destroy</u>. I <u>have come that they may have life</u>, and that they may have it more abundantly."
2. Fall of First Man, Adam.
    a. God commanded Adam not to eat the fruit of the tree of the knowledge of good and evil, "for in the day that you eat of it you shall surely die" (Genesis 2:17). But Adam and his wife Eve ate the fruit, and death came into man's spirit (Genesis 3:6-7).
    b. "Through one man sin entered the world, and death through sin, and thus death spread to all men, because all sinned..." (Romans 5:12). So Jesus, "the last Adam became a life-giving spirit" (1 Corinthians 15:45).

IV. Follow-Through.
1. "You are now born again, forgiven, and on your way to heaven." Show them that they are now the "righteousness of God" in Christ (2 Corinthians 5:17-21). Also share about their need to renew their minds (Romans 12:1-2).
2. Fill out a record card for the church and evangelism group follow up. Include their: name, address, phone number, and email. Set up a follow-up Bible study time within the next week or less. Invite them to come to church.

Notes and Reflections

Chapter 11

Godly Repentence

When you are leading someone to Christ, we want them to truly have Godly repentance and to be truly sorry for their sins.

This is a way you might speak to people about the sin issue when you are leading them to Christ:

> "Do you ever find yourself doing things that you really don't want to do. You're ashamed of doing those things and wish you could stop doing them. You've tried very hard to stop doing them, but haven't been able to stop. That's because we are living under the influence of a sin nature.
>
> The sin nature is why we need Jesus to be our Lord and Savior. It is only Jesus who gives us the strength to overcome the sin nature and all the sinful habits in our daily lives."

Here are some Scriptures to help you when you are witnessing about the importance of Godly repentance.

Acts 2:38 - Then Peter said to them, "Repent, and let every one of you be baptized in the name of Jesus Christ for the remission of sins; and you shall receive the gift of the Holy Spirit."

Acts 3:19 - "Repent therefore and be converted, that your sins may be blotted out, so that times of refreshing may come from the presence of the Lord."

2 Corinthians 7:10 - For godly sorrow produces repentance leading to salvation, not to be regretted; but the sorrow of the world produces death.

Hebrews 10:16-17 - "This is the covenant that I will make with them after those days, says the Lord: I will put My laws into their hearts, and in their minds I will write them," and then he adds, "Their sins and their lawless deeds I will remember no more."

Let the person you are witnessing to know that when they are truly sorry for their sins God erases them.

Notes and Reflections

102

Chapter 12

Steps to Baptism in the Holy Spirit

1. The Holy Spirit is the source of a Powerful Life.
   a. Acts 1:8. "Power"and abundant strength and ability to be an overcomer and live a victorious life.
   b. John 14:26. Comforter and teacher, Who helps you in your everyday life situations.
   c. Acts 19:1-2, 5-6. Baptism of the Holy Spirit is a separate experience from the work of the Holy Spirit in conversion.
   d. Acts 10:44-46. People were filled with the Holy Spirit and spoke in tongues.

2. What happens when you are filled with the Holy Spirit?
   Acts 2:4 - And they were all filled with the Holy Spirit, and began to speak with other tongues, as the Spirit gave them utterance.
The Holy Spirit is already here for every born again person. You do not need to wait for Him. Just ask to receive the Holy Spirit.
   Acts 2:38-39 - Then Peter said to them, "Repent, and let every one of you be baptized in the name of Jesus Christ for the remission of sins; and you shall receive the gift of the Holy Spirit.
   "For the promise is to you and to your children, and to all who are afar off, as many as the Lord our God will call."

3. Your mind won't understand or gain anything from speaking in tongues. (It will sound useless and foolish.) You are speaking mysteries to God, not to man.

a. 1 Corinthians 14:2 - For he who speaks in a tongue does not speak to men but to God, for no one understands him; however, in the spirit he speaks mysteries.

b. 1 Corinthians 14:14-15 - For if I pray in a tongue, my spirit prays, but my understanding is unfruitful. What is the conclusion then? I will pray with the spirit, and I will also pray with the understanding. I will sing with the spirit, and I will also sing with the understanding. (*Note:*Speaking in tongues is an act of your will. God will not force you to do it, or do it for you.)

4. If you ask for the Holy Spirit in faith, you will receive Him.

Luke 11:13 - "If you then, being evil, know how to give good gifts to your children, how much more will your heavenly Father give the Holy Spirit to those who seek Him."

5. Have the person ask for the Holy Spirit (Luke 11:13). Then lead them into a prayer inviting the Holy Spirit to fill them.

6. Pray for them. Let them know that they, as an act of faith, must open their mouth and let the Holy Spirit fill them.

7. Have them pray this prayer:

Father, I am asking you for the gift of the Holy Spirit.
Jesus, baptize me with the Holy Spirit and fire.
Dear Holy Spirit, come into me and fill me.

Boldly speak out in other tongues. Let the Holy Spirit just fill your mouth and use you.

Notes and Reflections

Chapter 13

The 48 Hour Principle

Follow up on new converts is a crucial key in discipling them.

> **Matthew 28:19-20 -** "Go therefore and make disciples of all the nations, baptizing them in the name of the Father and of the Son and of the Holy Spirit, teaching them to observe all things that I have commanded you; and lo, I am with you always, even to the end of the age."

The 48 Hour Principle tells us what we must do immediately after someon accepts Jesus as their Lord and Savior (regardless of whether this occurred at church, in a home, or during an outreach). All new converts need to be contacted within 48 hours of their conversion experience.

Here are some effective approaches to use when making contacts.

1. A visitation to their home. Take them a gift such as a Bible, praise CD's or a book which will help them in their spiritual growth.

2. Becoming a friend. Invite them out for coffee or tea, or do other things to encourage them to engage in a friendship.

3. Write to them. Send them an email or hand written personal note, with words of encouragement for them.

4. Call and invite them to church. Asking them to attend, or even to go with you, to a church service or special meeting often works well.

It is our responsibility to understand the crucial role of follow up in soul winning. New converts are spiritual children and it is our duty to pray for them and to stay in contact with them to the best of our ability.

This is especially crucial in the early stages, until they are established in the basic areas of their Christian walk such as prayer, Bible reading and church attendance.

Chapter 14

Adopt-A-Block

Adopt-A-Block is a project where outreach is focused upon one block or small area. Individuals and church ministry teams join together to effectively reach out with loving hearts and helping hands to those living in one block or small area near the church.

Adopt-A-Block involves doing such things as:
1. Yard work, baby sitting and cleaning houses.
2. Team-effort neighborhood cleanup.
3. Painting a house, fixing a roof, helping with remodeling.
4. Taking people small gifts, helping with spring planting, raking leaves, shoveling snow.
5. Bike repairs, minor car repairs, neighborhood car washes.
6. Teaching cooking, sewing, mechanics, nutrition, first aid
7. Job skills: resumes, interviewing techniques, computer basics, hair cutting and styling
8. Tutoring for children and adults

This list is endless. Ask the Lord to give you some creative ideas for your area, and list them below.

⇨_____

⇨_____

⇨_____

⇨_____

Find out what the talents are of people in your church and outreach groups and then use them to be a blessing and to assist people in the neighborhood near your church.

Chapter 15

Tips On Follow-Up

New converts need almost immediate follow up. Ideally and logically, the beginning follow up should come through the team members and church group who led the person to the Lord. These are the people who know who the convert is and how to contact them. They also have a relationship with the person, which was established when they led him or her to Jesus.

Twenty years ago Channel of Love Ministries put together Bible studies for new believers, covering the basics of the Christian faith. Those studies have been used in churches, homes, prisons, and nursing homes, to teach thousands of people.

Here's the contents of the newly revised book form of our course, *Now Is the Time Bible Studies.*

Your New Family	**God Cares for Your Needs**
New Creature	**You're Royalty**
The Holy Spirit and Power	**Healing is for Today**
The Word of God	**Why Witness**
How to Resist Your Enemy	**Assembling Together**
Fellowship with Our Father	**Why Be Baptized**

Why Study the Bible?
Yearly Bible Study Schedule
User Guidelines

The lessons work very well for new convert classes, small groups and in one-on-one situations. Many have also used them for youth, evangelism and discipleship classes.

This book is great for individuals too, as a way to renew and refresh their commitment to Jesus and His Church.

Members of evangelism teams should work through these studies in preparation for doing follow-up with new converts.

The Study book has easy to read lessons with fill-in answers and memory verses. The lessons are self-contained, and can be completed in an hour. Instructors need no special training. A yearly Bible Study is included. A Spanish Edition is available. Note the special materials to encourage reading through the whole Bible.

I. A Basic Follow-Up Plan

A. HOME BIBLE STUDIES

When a person accepts Jesus, set up a home Bible study with them. Ask them to choose the day and time which is most convenient for them and likely to have the fewest interruptions.

Tips: Write the appointment date on their calendar or in the booklet you leave with them. Make sure you have their correct name, address and phone number. Carry a Bible Study appointment book with you.

The study should be done by a trained leader, who understands that the convert is a new baby, born into the Kingdom of God. You need to work very closely with them for awhile.

Matthew 13:19-23 - "When anyone hears the word of the kingdom, and does not understand it, then the wicked one comes and snatches away what was sown in his heart. This is he who received seed by the wayside.

"But he who received the seed on stony places, this is he who hears the word and immediately receives it with joy; yet he has no root in himself, but endures only for a while. For when tribulation or persecution arises because of the word, immediately he stumbles.

"Now he who received seed among thorns is he who hears the word, and the cares of this world and the deceitfulness of riches choke the word, and he becomes unfruitful.

"But he who received seed on the good ground is he who hears the word and understands it, who indeed bears fruit and produces some a hundredfold, some sixty, some thirty."

B. PRAYER

We must pray and intercede for new converts so that Satan will not be able to steal the Word from them.

1. We have the power to bind and to loose.

> **Matthew 16:19 -** "And I will give you the keys of the kingdom of heaven, and whatever you bind on earth will be bound in heaven, and whatever you loose on earth will be loosed in heaven."

You must pull down anything that will hinder their study or their growth.

2. Start by praying them into the house of God. Ask them to come to church with you from time to time.

3. Pray this prayer for them:

> **Ephesians 1:17-20 -** That the God of our Lord Jesus Christ, the Father of glory, may give you the spirit of wisdom and revelation in the knowledge of Him, the eyes of your understanding being enlightened; that you may know what is the hope of His calling, what are the riches of the glory of His inheritance in the saints, and what is

the exceeding greatness of His power toward us who believe, according to the working of His mighty power which He worked in Christ when He raised Him from the dead and seated Him at His right hand in the heavenly places.

C. MAKE SURE THEY HAVE A BIBLE

The most important thing is that the person have a Bible for study. If they don't have one, buy one for them. What a gift of love!

D. BE THEIR FRIEND

You want the person you're discipling to have a rapport and relationship with you, and to become your friend.

II. Implementing the Basic Follow-up Plan.

A. HOME BIBLE STUDY — THE FIRST MEETING

You can take another person with you and work as a team. If you do this, one should do the talking, while the other works as a prayer supporter and helper.

Team teaching is not only good for the new convert, it allows an experienced teacher to prepare other Bible study teachers. A team member who has gone through a whole course program as an assistant instructor may then become a lead instructor for another convert.

Always start your study with an opening prayer.

Next, work through the lesson outline. Lessons should be 20 to 30 minutes, though you may go a bit longer, depending on the leading of the Spirit.

Tip: Don't overstay your visit. Sticking closely to the time you've set up helps establish you as being true to your word. If you stay too long, it may be your last visit.

At the end of the study, close in prayer and leave.

Tip: Stay on the topic of the lesson. New believers often have lots of questions and will try to get you off course. Explain that most questions will eventually be answered as you go through the lesson. Carry a notebook and jot down questions to answer later.

If they have a question you can't answer, let them know you don't know the answer. Tell them you're writing the item down and will get back to them with the answer as soon as possible.

Follow up on what you said. If you aren't able to locate an answer, ask for help from the pastor or another Christian at church. Call the convert to discuss what you've found out.

B. SOME WAYS TO BE A FRIEND

Remember: This person is an eternal soul and you must help them grow.

Drop them a note of encouragement or call them on the phone now and then.

Invite them to church, or to a Christian men's or women's meeting.

Try to get them into a group Bible study as soon as possible. They need Christian fellowship.

Don't get discouraged if once in awhile they just aren't home when you arrive for Bible Study.

Be patient with them; but be persistent. They need to develop a spiritual appetite.

They will grow as the Word of God goes into them each week, as you share the scriptures with them.

116

John 8:32 - "And you shall know the truth, and the truth shall make you free."

Remember what it was like when you first got saved. The new convert is a child of God. Let's treat them as such. We must love our neighbors as ourselves.

Luke 10:27 - So he answered and said, "You shall love the Lord your God with all your heart, with all your soul, and with all your strength, and with all your mind, and your neighbor as yourself."

Remember: We make disciples of people, not decisions for people.

Matthew 28:19 - "Go therefore and make disciples of all the nations, baptizing them in the name of the Father and of the Son and of the Holy Spirit, teaching them to observe all things that I have commanded you; and lo, I am with you always, even to the end of the age." Amen.

God bless you as you go about your Father's business.

John 4:34 - Jesus said to them, "My food is to do the will of Him who sent Me, and to finish His work."

Always pray for the person you are working with. Pray for the wisdom of God to be able to help them.

James 1:5-7 - If any of you lacks wisdom, let him ask of God, who gives to all liberally and without reproach, and it will be given to him.

But let him ask in faith, with no doubting, for he who doubts is like a wave of the sea driven and tossed by the wind.

Ask God for His special wisdom, as you disciple each new convert.

C. <u>MOVING TO A BIBLE STUDY OUTREACH</u>

Individual Bible study sessions often lead into a small group Bible study. After two or three one-on-one sessions, ask the new convert if they have a friend or two who might enjoy the lessons also. With your steady encouragement, some friends may start coming. As they begin being part of the new group, take time to lead them to Christ.

Once you've been doing door-to-door witnessing in an area, you may start having individual Bible studies happening in the same area on different days. After three or four meetings you can start grouping these new believers at one of their homes.

You might say: "Susie, we have been having studies at your home for three weeks now. Mary, who lives down the street, accepted Jesus just a week after you did. Would you mind if I invited Mary to join us here on Mondays to study with us?"

You'll find people will almost always say yes to moving to group studies.

Group Bible studies are very effective. New believers get the Word into them and also get to know one another. They can start reading the Bible together, going to church together, and supporting each other in many ways.

Important Note: Formally invite the new convert you're working with to go to church. When they say yes, check the time with them and if necessary arrange to pick them up. Generally people are nervous about going somewhere new by themselves.

When bringing a new convert to a Bible study or to church for the first time, go over the situation with them.

Discuss such things as the start and end times of the Service, what to bring (Bible, pen, notebook), how to dress, and child care needs. Tell them just a little bit about the meeting. Do whatever you can to make them relaxed and comfortable.

Notes and Reflections

Chapter 16

Discipleship Teams

Many church members are rooted and grounded in the Word, love God with all their hearts, and witness on their jobs. However they might never be interested in going witnessing door-to-door or in parks. This kind of person can be a great help to the soul-winning team.

Some soul winners love to go out and get people saved, while others like to disciple and teach new believers.

The soul winning team and the discipleship team need to work together. This helps both groups and also all those they minister to.

Discipleship people who want to help with soul winning should complete a 12-week study program, where they go over how to lead others into the baptism with the Holy Spirit, pray for the sick, and do one-on-one and small group Bible studies. *Now's The Time Bible Studies* has been designed for this purpose. See information and order form in the back of this book.

Part of the program should include having the discipleship person accompany the soul winning team member to some Bible studies.

When discipleship members complete the study program, their study leader should have them fill out an availability card. See the card in Appendix D.

122

Chapter 17

Visitation Ministry

Encourage all regular church members to bring people to church, especially those who are unsaved. Generally this process happens when church members visit their friends and neighbors, talk about the church, and ask people to come to a service.

I. Get People to Come to Church.

You must teach people what to say when they invite others to attend church. It's very helpful to have a church business card and printed announcement about an upcoming event at church, or a tract with the church information printed on it. Such items can be left with someone as reminders. Some things to include in your teaching are:

1. They must frequently encourage the person to come.

2. They must pray and intercede for the person, because Satan will put fear or obstacles in their path to keep them out of the House of God.

3. They must go pick the person up and bring them to church. Call them on Saturday night to remind them of the time and to be ready.

4. Inform the person you invite about what to wear, so they won't feel uncomfortable or embarrassed when they walk into church. Pick them up and bring them with you.

5. While you're taking them to church, talk with them about what to expect during your service. Remember, they may be nervous. Perhaps they have never been in a church, or they may be backslidden.

6. Some churches acknowledge those who are first-timers. Have them stand, and give them a visitor's packet. Having them stand, lets those on your Visitation Ministry see who they are and where they are sitting. Then they can seek them out after service and make them feel welcome.

7. The first-time visitor form in the packet should be filled out and placed in the offering. These forms go to the Visitation Ministry for follow up.

8. Altar Call. At the altar call time, suggest that your church members encourage their guests to come up. You should come and stand with them. After the altar call be sure all new converts fill out a follow up card (see sample in Appendix C).

9. Both first-time visitors and new converts should be visited that very next week by someone from the Visitation Ministry. At least they should receive a phone call. Remember what you read in Chapter 13: The 48-Hour Principle.

10. There should be a letter to all visitors from the pastor, which should also go out during that first week.

II. Home Visitation Ministry.

1. Become a friend. Ask the person about themselves.

2. Ask if they have any questions about the service that they would like answered.

3. Find out where they are from and a little bit about their family and church background.

4. Let them know the vision of your church, about your pastor, and about how you are involved in reaching the world for Jesus and meeting the needs of the people.

5. Ask them if they have any needs or prayer requests.

6. Make sure they are saved. If not, take time to lead them and their family to the Lord.

A good lead into a discussion about someone's salvation is to say: "Our biggest concern is to make sure everyone goes to heaven and has eternal life. Do you know that if you died right now, you would have eternal life with God in heaven?

If they answer yes, they are sure about their salvation, ask them to tell you their testimony just to be certain. Remember that many people think just going to church or being a good person is how you receive eternal life.

7. Once you know the person is saved, encourage them to move into a deeper walk with God.

8. Explain the various kinds of activities at your church, such as Bible Studies, adult and children's Sunday School, outreaches and programs.

9. If the person is not saved, lead them to the Lord and then set up a regular Bible study time with them, using study guides. Or immediately get them involved in a new convert class.

Notes and Reflections

Chapter 18

How To Handle Objections

When you are sharing the Gospel, you will hear lots of objections. You need to realize where these are coming from. Do not take the objections as a personal affront to you. Satan does not want anyone to be saved. Therefore he will put all kinds of objections in people's minds.

> **Ephesians 6:12 -** For we do not wrestle against flesh and blood, but against principalities, against powers, against the rulers of darkness of this age, against spiritual hosts of wickedness in the heavenly places.

> **2 Corinthians 4:3-4 -** But if our gospel is veiled, it is veiled to those who are perishing, whose minds the god of this age has blinded, who do not believe, lest the light of the gospel of the glory of Christ, who is the image of God, should shine on them.

It is important to be able to answer commonly asked questions from the scriptures. Try to answer objections as briefly as possible. Then get on with telling them THE GOOD NEWS!

Some of the Most Common Objections With their Answers

1. I believe I'm going to heaven. After all I am a church member and have attended church all my life.

That's wonderful! Have you ever asked Jesus to be Lord of your life? You probably believe in Jesus, but you have to have a personal relationship with Him.

> **John 3:3 -** "...unless one is born again, he cannot see the kingdom of God."
> **Titus 3:5 -** ...not by works of righteousness which we have done, but according to His mercy He saved us....
> **Romans 3:10 -** As it is written: "There is none righteous, no, not one...."
> **John 3:16 -** "For God .... gave His only begotten Son, that whoever believes in Him should not perish...."

2. Things about God and the Bible seem foolish to me.

> **1 Corinthians 1:18-21 -** For the message of the cross is foolishness to those who are perishing....
> **1 Corinthians 1:27 -** But God has chosen the foolish things of the world to put to shame the wise....

3. There are too many hypocrites in the church.

I agree with you. Do you know that even Jesus had trouble with hypocrites during His days on earth? But just as you don't call all store clerks "grumps" because you know one bad clerk, so we shouldn't call everyone in the church a hypocrite.

Matthew 6:5-18 - "And when you pray, you shall not be like the hypocrites. For they love to pray standing in the synagogues and on the corners of the street, that they might be seen by men...."

Luke 11:43-44 - "Woe to you Pharisees! For you love the best seats in the synagogues and greetings in the marketplaces. Woe to you scribes...."

4. If God loves everyone so much, why is the world so messed up?

John 10:10 - "The thief does not come except to steal, and to kill, and to destroy. I have come that they may have life, and that they may have it more abundantly."

Romans 5:12-21 - Therefore, just as through one man sin entered the world, and death through sin, and thus death spread to all men, because all sinned...

James 1:17 - Every good gift and every perfect gift is from above, and comes down from the Father of lights, with whom there is no variation or shadow of turning.

5. I can't understand the Bible.

1 Corinthians 2:14 - But the natural man does not receive the things of the Spirit of God....

2 Corinthians 4:3-4 - But even if our gospel is veiled, it is veiled to those who are perishing....

John 3:3 - "...unless one is born again he cannot see the kingdom of God."

6. Will God really care for me?

Yes, He will. Once you have accepted Jesus as your personal Savior and have made Him Lord of your life, you become part of the family of God, and your Heavenly Father is committed to you!

Matthew 6:25-31 - "....Now if God so clothes the grass of the field, which today is, and to-morrow is thrown into the oven, will He not much more clothe you, O you of little faith?"

Philippians 4:19 - And my God shall supply all your need according to His riches in glory by Christ Jesus.

7. I don't believe in Heaven or Hell.

The Bible teaches that there are both places. Most people don't want to believe in Hell, because they don't want to go there. Wouldn't you rather go to heaven?

2 Peter 2:4 - For if God did not spare the angels who sinned, but cast them down to hell and delivered them into chains of darkness....

Matthew 25:41 - "Then He will also say to those on the left hand, 'Depart from Me, you cursed, into the everlasting fire prepared for the devil and his angels...'"

You see, hell was never created for man, but for the devil and his angels. We can choose not to go there, simply by asking Jesus into our life.

Other scriptures to read are:

Psalm 9:17: The wicked shall be turned into hell, and all the nations that forget God.

Luke 12:5: "...Fear Him who, after He has killed, has power to cast into hell...."

Luke 16:25: "But Abraham said, 'Son, remember that in your lifetime you received your good things, and likewise Lazarus evil things; but now he is comforted and you are tormented."

Revelation 14:10: ...He shall be tormented with fire and brimstone in the presence of the holy angels and in the presence of the Lamb.

Revelation 21:8: But the cowardly, unbelieving, abominable...shall have their part in the lake which burns with fire....

8. I believe God is just and we go the Heaven.

I'm really glad you brought that up. God is love, and it's also true that:

Romans 3:23 - ...all have sinned and fall short of the glory of God.

Romans 6:23 - For the wages of sin is death.

John 3:3 - Jesus answered and said to him, "Most assuredly, I say to you, unless one is born again, he cannot see the kingdom of God."

9. I don't believe in this resurrection stuff. I believe that when you die, it's all over.

Lots of people believe this. That way they don't have to face the possibility that they might have to account for the deeds they did during their lifetime.

1 Corinthians 15:42 - So also is the resurrection of the dead. The body is sown in corruption, it is raised in incorruption.

1 Corinthians 15:50-53 - Now this I say, brethren, that flesh and blood cannot inherit the kingdom of God; nor does corruption inherit incorruption....

John 11:25 - Jesus said to her, "I am the resurrection and the life. He who believes in Me, though he may die, he shall live."

So you see, there **is** a resurrection. And the only sure way to be part of the resurrection which leads to eternal life with our Heavenly Father is by choosing now to accept Jesus as Savior and Lord of your life.

10. I'm young, and I have lots of time. I'll think about getting saved later.

Proverbs 27:1 - Do not boast about tomorrow, for you do not know what a day may bring forth.

2 Corinthians 6:2 - ...Behold, now is the accepted time; behold, now is the day of salvation.

By not making a decision, you will remain in the kingdom of darkness.

John 3:19 - "...light has come into the world, and men loved darkness rather than light...."

Can you really afford not to make a decision today? What is the price of your soul?

11. I have sinned so much in my life that I don't believe God could ever forgive me.

Isaiah 1:18 - "Come now, let us reason together," says the Lord, "though your sins are like scarlet, they shall be as white as snow; though they are red like crimson, they shall be as wool."

Romans 5:6-8 - For when we were still without strength, in due time Christ died for the ungodly....while we were still sinners, Christ died for us.

Galatians 1:4 - who gave Himself for our sins...."

2 Corinthians 5:17 - Therefore, if anyone is in Christ, he is a new creation; old things have passed away; behold, all things are new.

1 John 2:12 - I write to you, little children, because your sins are forgiven you for His name's sake.

12. I have tried reading the Bible, but it doesn't make any sense to me. I can't understand what I read.

1 Corinthians 2:14 - But the natural man does not receive the things of the Spirit of God....

2 Corinthians 4:3-4 - But even if our gospel is veiled, it is veiled to those who are perishing, whose minds the god of this age has blinded, who do not believe lest the light of the gospel of the glory of Christ, who is the image of God, should shine on them.

You see, the Bible is the inspired Word of God, and it cannot be understood by the natural man.

The Spirit of God has to be dwelling within us to help us understand what God says in His word.

13. How can I know for sure that I have eternal life?

Romans 10:13- For whoever calls on the Lord shall be saved.

Romans 10:9-10 - that if you confess with your mouth the Lord Jesus and believe in your heart that God has raised Him from the dead, you will be saved. For with the heart man believeth....

1 John 5:11 - And this is the testimony: that God has given us eternal life, and this life is in His Son.

1 John 5:12 - He who has the Son has life; he who does not have the Son of God does not have life.

1 John 5:13 - These things I have written to you who believe in the name of the Son of God, that you may know that you have eternal life, and that you may continue to believe in the name of the Son of God.

Notes and Reflections

138

Chapter 19

Some Ways To Stay Faithful In Soul Winning

Keep a Follow-Through Chart.

Being a soul-winner involves faithfulness. Once you get someone saved, you need to see that they are followed up so that they can grow and develop in the things of God.

Take the time to follow up personally with each one whom you lead to the Lord.

   1. Pray that Christ be formed in them.

   2. Take the time to teach them in a small Bible Study.

   3. Take them to Church.

   4. Pay them a visit, give them a phone call, or send them an email.

   5. Keep in touch with them often, so that the seeds can take root.

     Note: Other people on the soul-winning and discipleship team may do parts of the follow up at times, but it is important for you, as the soul-winner, to keep a record, to assure that things get done, and that no one is accidently overlooked.

140

The checklist on the opposite page is something you might use to keep a record of your follow up with an individual.

The Holy Spirit Will
Put People in Your Path!

Pray that doors will open so that you can preach Jesus to them. Pray that Christ will be formed in each person.

Ask God:
What is the problem with this person?
When do you want me to to do something concern ing them?
What do you want me to say to them?

If the Holy Spirit brings a person's name into your mind, that means that God is especially working on that person right then.

Follow-Up Checklist

For follow-up with individuals (Home visit, Bible Study, special prayer, bringing to church or meeting, etc.). Record date, activity, and brief note or reminder.

**Name (Address Zip Code Email Phone)

_____

_____

Date   Notes

_____   _____

_____   _____

_____   _____

_____   _____

**Name (Address Zip Code Email Phone)

_____

_____

Date   Notes

_____   _____

_____   _____

_____   _____

_____   _____

**Name (Address Zip Code Email Phone)

_____

_____

Date   Notes

_____   _____

_____   _____

_____   _____

_____   _____

**Name (Address Zip Code Email Phone)

_____

_____

Date   Notes

_____   _____

_____   _____

_____   _____

_____   _____

What if...

multiple churches and groups came together
with a God-given vision
and carried through with a God-given plan
for taking their city for Jesus?

This additional chapter is added to Let's Go Fishing! to encourage and inform those seeking how to share the salvation message and effectively disciple masses of people at one time.

The rest of the book teaches and reaffirms the Gospel message: All are called to go into the world and share about Jesus. Yet the Bible is very clear. Jesus wants us to do much more than any one person or group could think of or imagine.

Jesus said to take the whole message of the Gospel to the whole world. This is a large project! It requires that people take to heart one of Jesus' last prayers, recorded in John 17:21: "that they all may be one, as You, Father, are in Me, and I in You, that they also may be one in Us, that the world may believe that You sent Me."

God is Taking the City is a vision and plan for impacting cities for Jesus. It's focus is to reach everyone in the city on the same day, using media, events and every possible means to share Jesus.

On the day of Pentecost, 120 people were "in one accord" in an upper room. They had gone there days before, dismayed, discouraged and somewhat defeated. Then on that day the Holy Spirit empowered them with God's power, grace and authority. By the end of that day over 3,000 people from many places had given their lives to Jesus.

Take this event to heart; it was written for our encouragement and our example!

Chapter 20

God Is Taking the City

The Purpose

- To equip all the saints to do the ministry of evangelism as commanded by Jesus, who commissioned us all to go throughout the world preaching the Gospel.

- To teach and establish outreach ministry to reach the lost and destitute in our cities through ongoing, effectual ministry as established by Jesus to feed, clothe and care for the lonely, broken, and imprisoned.

- To effectually reach every soul in our cities, assuring that each one is given an opportunity to know Jesus – creating real church growth for the glory of God's kingdom.

- To teach and train the saints in spiritual warfare, to the pulling down of real strongholds in real places where they live.

- To assure the ongoing, long-lasting success of outreach and evangelism by making these things a part of our lifestyle. This would be done by practical application teaching and training in key areas of ministry, where people can get repetitive, hands-on experience.

- To create ways to mobilize each member of a church, aiding and encouraging them to realize their positions in the Body of Christ.

God is Taking the City
Where do we start?

A. Train the saints. 2 Timothy 2: 2. What you have heard, impart to faithful men who will be able to teach others. Train leaders in all aspects of outreach ministry: food, clothing, music, and outreach activities.

B. Motivate. Ephesians 4:16. The whole body is held together by that which every joint supplies, according to the proper working of each part, causing the growth of the body for the building up of itself in love. Motivate the saints to evangelize everyone in your city and area with the Gospel so that the saving love of Jesus can abound for all.

C. Teach new converts. Matthew 28:19-20. Make disciples of all nations....teaching them to observe all that Jesus commanded. Every convert needs to be trained to go back into the harvest and bring in others.

D. Follow up with new converts. John 8:31-32. Disciples of Jesus are ones who abide in His word. It is His truth that sets people free. Effective follow up means keeping in contact, prayerfully encouraging, and being there for those who are new or still weak in their faith.

E. Organize team ministry. Acts 2:40-47. Peter took in the first believers and taught them to live, work, and pray together, praising God and living in an orderly way, knowing the power of submission. Organize teams using New Testament principles where each member learns the value of submitting to each other.

F.   Actively share a common vision. Romans 12:4-5. There are many members in one body, but all the members do not have the same function. The members are one body in Christ, and individually members one of another. Build a network of ministries working together with a common vision.

G.   Labor together. Luke 10:17. After Jesus sent them to preach the Gospel, the 70 returned joyfully, proclaiming "Lord, even the demons obey us when we use your name!"
    Laboring together causes a bond, with strong relationships being formed within a church family.

H. Build Relationships. 1 Corinthians 12:12. The human body is one member with many members; so also is the body of Christ. Work with a vision of unity in mind, so that even the littlest effort will be seen in the light of a big future.

I.   Continually reinforce the team-church idea.   Paul wrote about his constant prayer for those in a church he had ministered in some time before. He lets them know he still has a personal interest in their growth, welfare and accomplishments. This is an attitude that truly assures long term church growth and vitality.

Long after the launch of God is Taking the City, the effect of the teaching, training and teamwork will go on and on!

APPENDIX A

Questionnaires For Witnessing

Copy and use these for door-to-door witnessing. Carefully fill out the bottom for use in follow-up.

Remember, the questionnaires are just a guide. It is always wise to ask the Holy Spirit to lead us about exactly what to say and do in each situation.

There are separate forms for adults and teenagers. We suggest adjusting their size and copying them two to a page on 8 ½ x 11 paper. Narrower forms are easy to carry and to handle while witnessing.

Questionnaire... General

We're in your neighborhood to find out how to be of service in our Community. We have a short questionnaire that will only take a few minutes to fill out. May we come in?

1. What is the thing you'd most like to see changed:

in   neighborhood._____

in   world._____

2. What is your religious background?
   Catholic   Protestant   Other_____

3. How often do you attend Church?
   Weekly   Often   Sometimes   Never

4. In what ways does your church reach out into the community?

_____

5. If you were to die today, do you know if you would be in Heaven?

_____

6. If you were standing before God, and God said to you, "Why should I let you into Heaven?" What would you say?

_____

**Share Jesus with them, and how you can know for sure
that you will go to Heaven. Share the Gospel.**

Name_____

Address_____

email_____

Phone (area code)_____

   ☐ **Salvation**   ☐ **Baptism Holy Spirit**
   ☐ **Bible Study** (Set date/time for visitation)

Day/Date_____   **Time**_____

Comments:

_____

Team Names & Phone   **Date:**_____
1._____
2._____

A Questionnaire... For Teens

We're interested in getting opinions from teens about things that could help you. How can we be of service to help you or other teens? We have a short questionnaire and it will only take a few minutes to fill out.

1. What is the thing you'd most like to see changed, to help teens?
_____

2. Do you know anyone in your area who is suicidal? _____
_____

3. Do you know any people who have gotten into Satanism? _____
_____

4. Why do you think people are hurting?
_____

5. What is your religious background? (circle)
    Catholic   Protestant
Other_____
_____

6. How often do you attend Church? (circle)
      Weekly   Often   Sometimes   Never
_____

7. What do you think about where you would be if you died? _____
_____

8. Suppose you were standing before God, and God said to you, "Why should I let you into Heaven?" What would you say?
_____

Name_____

Address_____

email_____

Phone (area code)_____
      ☐ **Salvation**   ☐ **Baptism Holy Spirit**
      ☐ **Bible Study** (Set date/time for visitation)
Day/Date_____   **Time**_____
Comments:
_____
Team Names & Phone   **Date:**_____

1._____
2._____

LET'S GO FISHING!, Joan Pearce, Channel of Love Ministries - www.joanpearce.org.

Copyright © 2008. May be duplicated for evangelistic purposes, provided not for resale.

APPENDIX B

New Convert Record Form

This form is designed to be used for follow-up. Complete a form for each new convert when they are saved. Make copies, to distribute to: 1: Personal Worker for that Convert, 2: Soul-Winner team member, 3: Church records, 4: Church Intercessory Prayer Group.

NEW CONVERT RECORD

Name _____ Date_____

Address _____

City _____State_____ Zip Code_____

Phone _____E-mail_____

WITNESS TEAM

Name_____

Phone _____ E-mail_____

Name_____

Phone _____ E-mail_____

DISCIPLESHIP WORKER

Name_____

Phone _____ E-mail_____

COMMENTS

_____

_____

_____

APPENDIX C
REFERRAL CARD
FOR FOLLOW-UP

This card can be used by church members who wish to refer a friend, relative or neighbor to the church for follow-up. The cards can be distributed to the Visitation Minister, Witnessing Minister, or whoever is most appropriate.

Often people feel inadequate to witness to their friends, or perhaps they know shut-ins or people who are in the hospital who could use an extra visitor or two.

Before going to visit, contact whoever turned in the referral card, to learn about the person you're going to see. Have the person who made the referral go with you on the first visit. This will help put the one visited at ease, and it will also help them learn how to minister to others.

FOLLOW-UP REFERRAL CARD

*REFERRED TO:_____Date_____

<u>Person Referred:</u> _____Date:_____

Address: _____

_____
City   State   Zip Code

Phone _____   Email_____

    Person Needs:

___ Salvation   ___ Healing   ___ Holy Spirit   ___ Other

(Explain)_____

*REFERRED BY: _____

Address:_____

_____
City   State   Zip Code

Phone _____   Email_____

LET'S GO FISHING!, Joan Pearce, Channel of Love Ministries - www.joanpearce.org.
Copyright © 2008. May be duplicated for evangelistic purposes, provided not for resale.

APPENDIX D

Use this form to keep a record of discipleship team members who are available to do follow-up on new converts. See Chapter 16 for information on organizing Discipleship Teams.

Discipleship Team Members

Name   (Please Print)

_____

_____

Address

_____

City   State   Zip Code

_____

Email

Phone

_____

Home   Work/cell phone

Days Available (circle)

Mon   Tues   Wed   Thurs   Fri   Sat   Any

Times Available (circle)

Mornings   Afternoons   Evenings   Any

Comments

_____

_____

About Channel of Love Ministries

Evangelist Joan Pearce was radically saved in 1977, and shortly afterwards moved to Washington State. There she was greatly inspired and discipled by the daughter and son-in-law of the late Evangelist John G. Lake. God asked Joan to step out and do a home Bible Study, even though she couldn't read.

Joan recognized God's hand was on her, and that He was calling her into ministry. Her heart cry is for souls and to fulfill Luke 4:18–19, "to preach the gospel to the poor," heal the brokenhearted, and bring healing and freedom to the hurting and oppressed – "to proclaim the acceptable year of the Lord."

Today Joan continues in full-time ministry, traveling across the United States and overseas. Channel of Love Ministries is doing "God is Taking the City" campaigns, where Joan and her husband Marty are seeing churches come together in unity to evangelize their cities. Joan also does revivals, church meetings, and city-wide crusades where thousands come to Jesus. Part of her ministry is to teach practical evangelism classes and to conduct Holy Spirit Miracle Services where there are many notable and creative miracles. She and Marty have a heart to feed and clothe the needy and have ministered to the poor throughout the world.

Joan is on TV across the United States, and is on the internet world wide. The Channel of Love Ministries website is **www.joanpearce.org.** She and Marty are fulfilling God's great commission to "Go into all the world and preach the gospel" (Mark 16:15.)

Contacting Channel of Love Ministries
www.joanpearce.org

▶ To write us a note, praise report or prayer request

▶ Learn more about our ministry and its goals

▶ Receive more details about God is Taking the City (see Chapter 20)

▶ Offer financial and practical support

▶ See our current schedule

▶ Learn about opportunities to participate in Channel of Love Ministries trips

▶ Get information on scheduling meetings for your church or group

▶ Order books, CD's and DVD's

▶ Sign up for our free Newsletter

▶ Download our free ministry helps

▶ ...and much more

We look forward to hearing from you!

Channel of Love Ministries Intl.

*Helping you to grow spiritually and
share your faith more effectively!*

Yes, YOU can hear GOD too!
Order No. 0007-B
Price $15.00

Every believer has the right to hear from Heaven. This down to earth book will challenge **you** to hear from God!

Let's Go Fishing!
Order No. 0042-B
Price $15.00

Are you wondering? "What's God's purpose and plan for my life?" "How do I: Draw my loved ones and others to the Lord.... Answer their questions.... Help my church or group reach out to the lost and needy?" This book answers your questions.

Now's the Time Bible Studies
Order No. 0043-B
Price $10.00

Here are precious keys for unlocking and releasing God-given provision, power and authority into your life, and experiencing the precious love of Jesus. You'll grow spiritually -- and be able to share what you've learned with others.

The Empty Spot
Order No. 0045-B
Price per pkg. of 10 $12.00

An excellent booklet for getting people saved and for discipling those who have recently received Jesus. This book has led thousands to Jesus. It's a great witnessing tool!

BOOK ORDER FORM

You can also order on our website: **www.joanpearce.org**

Special orders or **quantity orders**: contact us at our website or by phone.

Cat. #	Description	Price	Qty	Sub-Total
<u>0007-B</u>	**Yes, You Can Hear GOD, too!**	**$15.00**		
<u>0042-B</u>	**Let's Go Fishing!**	**$15.00**		
<u>0043-B</u>	**Now's the Time Bible Studies**	**$10.00**		
<u>0045-B</u>	**Empty Spot - Pkg. of 10**	**$12.00**		

Please allow 2-3 weeks for delivery	**Sub-Total**	
<u>Mail Order Form and payment to:</u> **Channel of Love Ministries, Intl.** **PO Box 458** **Red Bluff, CA 96080** **877-852-6194 (office)**	**<u>S/H</u>** Add 30% of Sub-Total	
	<u>Total</u>	

❑   **Payment enclosed**   ❑   **MasterCard**   ❑   **VISA**

Card # _____   **Exp.** _____

Phone #_____**Signature** _____
(Req.)

Name_____

Address_____

_____

City_____**State**_____

ZIP_____**EMail**_____